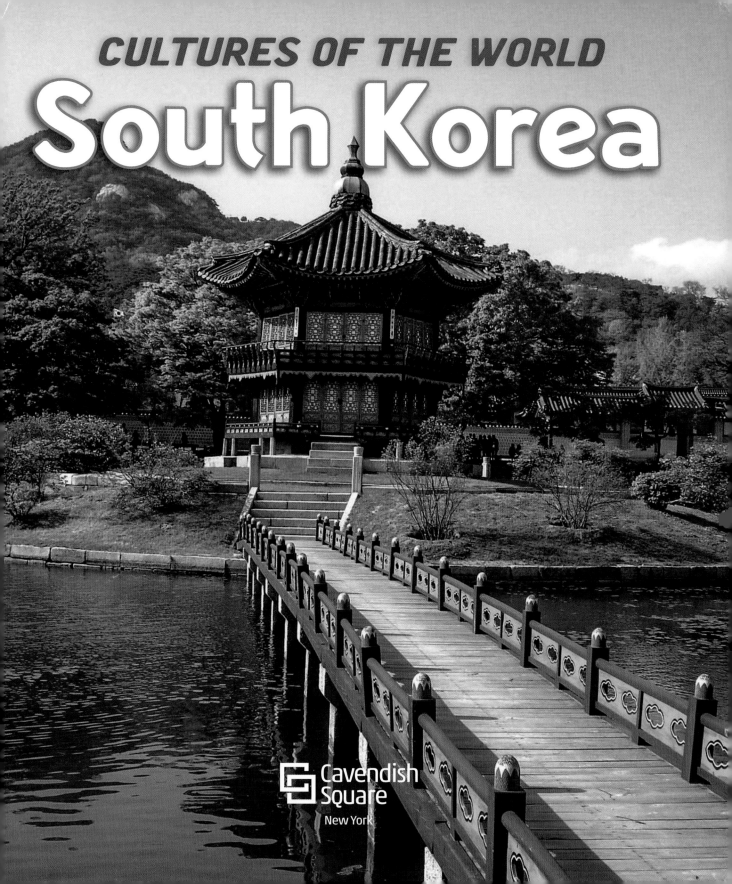

CULTURES OF THE WORLD
South Korea

Cavendish
Square

New York

Published in 2015 by Cavendish Square Publishing, LLC
243 5th Avenue, Suite 136, New York, NY 10016

Copyright © 2015 by Cavendish Square Publishing, LLC

Third Edition

Website: cavendishsq.com

This publication represents the opinions and views of the author based on his or her personal experience, knowledge, and research. The information in this book serves as a general guide only. The author and publisher have used their best efforts in preparing this book and disclaim liability rising directly or indirectly from the use and application of this book.

CPSIA Compliance xzInformation: Batch #WW15CSQ

All websites were available and accurate when this book was sent to press.

Library of Congress Cataloging-in-Publication Data
DuBois, Jill, 1952-
  South Korea / Jill Dubois, Debbie Nevins.
    pages cm. — (Cultures of the world)
  Includes bibliographical references and index.
  ISBN 978-1-50260-079-0 (hardcover) ISBN 978-1-50260-083-7 (ebook)
  1. Korea (South)—Juvenile literature. I. Nevins, Debbie. II. Title.

DS907.4.D83 2015
951.95—dc23

                        2014032332

Writers, Jill Dubois; Debbie Nevins, third edition
Editor, third edition: Debbie Nevins
Art Director, third edition: Jeffrey Talbot
Designer, third edition: Jessica Nevins
Production Manager, third edition: Jennifer Ryder-Talbot
Cover Picture Researcher: Amy Greenan
Picture Researcher, third edition: Jessica Nevins

PRECEDING PAGE
An inviting scene on Emperor Island.

Printed in the United States of America

CONTENTS

SOUTH KOREA TODAY

KOREA. SOUTH KOREANS CALL IT HANGUK; NORTH KOREANS call it Choson. Korea was once one nation but now it is two. And there could hardly be two more different countries than today's North Korea and South Korea. The contrast is stunning, given that both nations emerged from the same people with the same history and culture. The two present a fascinating study of the effects of opposing systems of government—North Korea is a repressive, totalitarian, communist state, while South Korea is a vibrant democracy—but the comparison is tempered by the sadness of the situation. In the partitioning of Korea in 1948, people's lives were broken; families were permanently separated, with brothers and sisters, parents and children prevented from ever being together again.

In the nineteenth century, Korea was often called "the Hermit Kingdom" because it was cut off from the rest of world—and perhaps, charmingly behind the times. Today that term is sometimes used to refer to North Korea, but the implication is far from quaint.

Isolated and literally fenced off from the world, North Korea is considered a rogue state, a nation that operates without regard for international law and one

A crowded street in Seoul, South Korea, bustles with people and attractions.

which poses a threat to the security of other nations. In this case, the nation most threatened by North Korea is South Korea. The constant barrage of belligerence from the North has left the South Koreans wearily inclined to shrug off such threats as mere bluster. But the South Korean government knows it cannot afford to be nonchalant about its aggressive neighbor.

Other recently divided countries (meaning divided less than a century ago), such as Ireland and Northern Ireland or India and Pakistan, have problematic relationships to be sure. But none are as starkly dissimilar as the Koreas. Yet many Koreans hold out the hope of eventual reunification—but on whose terms?

For the most part, this book is about the Republic of Korea (ROK), the democracy that occupies the southern half of the Korean Peninsula. South Korea is a land of contrasts in itself. It emerged from the Korean War in tatters as a poor, rural, backward country. Today it is among the wealthiest, most advanced of nations—an economic powerhouse—boasting the world's hardest workers and highest achieving students. It is also a relatively safe place, with a crime rate lower than that of other countries with a comparable economic status. South Korea has spawned an energetic and appealing youth pop culture, with music, dance, and fashion celebrities attracting millions of fans across Asia and beyond.

South Korea has great natural beauty: majestic mountain ranges, idyllic islands, and nearly 1,500 miles (2,413 km) of coastline. It also has lively cities with glittering shopping emporiums and high-tech transportation systems side by side ancient art and architecture. In manufacturing, South Korea's top brands, such as Hyundai, Samsung, and LG, are industry leaders worldwide.

Yet South Koreans cling to traditions and ways of thinking that date back centuries or even millennia. Remnants of ancient shamanistic religion color much of modern life, mixing comfortably with the ancient Confucian philosophy that guides personal as well as national behavior.

The Confucian culture esteems filial piety, humaneness, and ritual—that is, respect for parents and the elderly, kindness, and social order. In Korean society, these values are expressed in family rituals and social traditions. For example, a string of dried red peppers strung across the front door of a Korean home signifies the recent birth of a boy. Arranged marriages are still customary (though not as much as in the past), an indicator of filial piety in honoring the parents' choice of a spouse. Young people also venerate the elderly and would never act casually or sloppily around an older person.

Confucian thought is also seen in Koreans' public behavior. According to Confucianism, repressing emotion is a sign of culture. Hugging and kissing, or engaging in other public displays of affection are strictly bad manners. Even holding hands in public is frowned upon. Many formal rules dictate social behavior, from bowing to table manners to body language.

Koreans value peacefulness and harmony above all, and yet they are very driven. They work hard at self-improvement—physical appearance is extremely important—and push themselves doggedly at work and in school. The push for perfection results in high achievement but also stress, and unfortunately, high rates of suicide. For at least eight consecutive years in the twenty-first century, South Korea has had the highest suicide rate in

South Korean women wearing traditional costumes perform a memorial dance.

A young woman relaxes in the hot thermal spa water pool of the Seorak Waterpia aquapark in Sokcho.

the industrialized world. In 2012, at least 14,160 people committed suicide, an average of thirty-nine people per day. That dire statistic is more than double what it was in 2000. Suicide is the leading cause of death for people between the ages of ten and thirty in South Korea.

South Koreans even work hard at relaxing. Bath houses called *jimjilbang* are vital to a person's well-being. These facilities provide vigorous, state-of-the-art spa treatments that go well beyond what even the most pampered Westerners are accustomed to. Another form of relaxation, drinking, is a culture unto itself. When considering only hard liquor consumption (as opposed to wine and beer) studies find that South Koreans top the list worldwide. The Koreans' fondness for the fermented rice spirit *soju* is the main motivator for that dubious achievement—that, and the attitude expressed in the common Korean saying, "He who drinks more works better."

In this culture, a playful inventiveness bumps up against a stubborn conformity to rigid standards. The ROK's bubbly pop culture and love for the ultra modern coexist with its more restrictive social mores. The Korean people's ethnic pride in their homogeneity—South Korea is almost 100 percent ethnically Korean—can also reveal itself as racism and discrimination toward other peoples.

As South Korea moves forward through the twenty-first century, it faces many challenges. Uppermost are the fragile relationships it has with North Korea, its "evil twin," and Japan, its former oppressor. Beyond those, the ROK has so much to offer the world that it can't afford to remain cocooned by old "Hermit Kingdom" attitudes. This vibrant country needs to learn how to

treasure and preserve its identity and customs while yet opening its arms to the world. Attitudes about racial purity and such are rapidly becoming outmoded in today's fast-paced world.

Korea has long seen itself as a tiger. Indeed, tigers once lived in abundant numbers on the peninsula. The culture's creation myth includes a tiger that wishes to become human, but proves too impatient to complete the grueling requirements. And so he roams the mountains as a shadowy but sacred guardian. To the Koreans, the tiger is a symbol of courage, strength, and dignity, but the tiger is also fierce. No doubt it was that ferocious nature that drove the South Koreans to transform their nation from the world's poorest to one of the richest in a mere fifty years. Now, the South Korean Tiger must consider its next move. The world is watching.

A monk and a tiger sit side by side in this Korean painting.

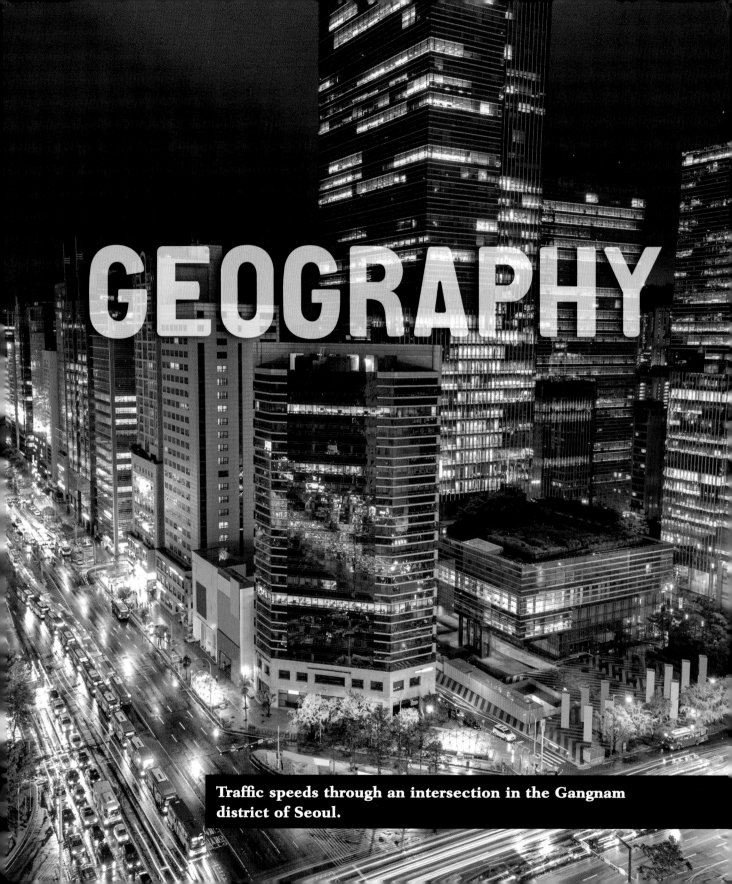

GEOGRAPHY

Traffic speeds through an intersection in the Gangnam district of Seoul.

1

SOME SAY THE KOREAN PENINSULA is shaped like a tiger. Others say it resembles a rabbit. In Korea, both the tiger and the rabbit are important symbols that are found in folktales and folk art. The contrast and tension between the tiger and the rabbit—aggression and submission— has meaning in the history of the Korean Peninsula.

One poetic interpretation of the name *Korea* is "Land of High Mountains and Sparkling Streams."

A view from space shows the Korean Peninsula reaching out toward the islands of Japan.

Whichever animal it conjures, if any, the peninsula is a chunk of land jutting off the eastern part of continental Asian. It extends some 684 miles (1,100 km) into the Pacific Ocean. It reaches southward from China and Russia into the East Sea, or Sea of Japan. It is positioned between the same latitudes as the area between Vermont and South Carolina. Korea is surrounded by water on three sides: the Korea Bay and the Yellow Sea to the west, the Korea Strait to the south, and the East Sea to the east. There are more than 3,400 islands along the coast.

The Korean peninsula consists of two political units, the Democratic People's Republic of Korea, or North Korea, and the Republic of Korea, or South Korea. The two are divided by a line 38 degrees north of the Equator. North Korea occupies 55 percent of the peninsula's 84,402 square miles (218,600 square km) of land.

Korea's name comes from the Goryeo dynasty, which ruled the peninsula from 918 to 1392. The name *Goryeo* means "high and clear"—an appropriate description of the high peaks and clear streams that characterize Korea's terrain. Korea is also often called the Land of the Morning Calm for its pretty and peaceful sunrise scenes.

A sunrise in South Korea gives meaning to the name "Land of the Morning Calm."

TOPOGRAPHY

The terrain of the Korean peninsula is dominated by highlands. In North Korea, the Kaema Plateau covers land in the center and east, while the Hamgyong Mountains extend northeast.

Korea's highest mountain, Mount Baektu, is located in the region of the Hamgyong range, near the Chinese border. The extinct volcano contains a large lake in its crater, 9,003 feet (2,743 m) above sea level.

Smaller ranges in North Korea include the Kangnam Mountains, which stretch across the northwest, and the Nangnim and Myohyang ranges in the center.

The Taebaek Mountains, which extend into South Korea, include *Kumgang*, or "Diamond Mountain," a peak so beloved it has a different name for each season. Kumgang is 5,377 feet (1,638 m) tall and is famous for its scenery, as is *Seorak* ("Snowy Peak"), a peak in the South Korean section of the Taebaek

Fog creeps up the slopes of Seorak Mountain.

range. Seorak's highest peak, at 5,604 feet (1,708 m) above sea level, divides the mountain into the eastern Outer Seorak and the western Inner Seorak.

The Sobaek Mountains are located farther south. On Jeju, the largest island of the Korean peninsula, is South Korea's highest peak, Halla, at 6,398 feet (1,949 m).

RIVERS AND CRATER LAKES

Many of Korea's rivers are short and fast and drain into the Yellow Sea. North Korea's longest rivers begin at Mount Baektu and flow along the border with China. The Yalu courses 491 miles (790 km) west and drains into the Korea Bay, while the Tumen runs 324 miles (521 km) northeast and drains into the East Sea.

The Imjin flows 158 miles (254 km) into South Korea, where it meets the 319-mile (514-km) Han, South Korea's second longest river after the Naktong, which is 324 miles (521 km) long. The Naktong and the Han are tapped to supply water for industry and irrigation.

Korea's most famous lakes are volcanic crater lakes at Mount Baektu and Mount Halla. There is no volcanic activity on the peninsula, but there are hot springs and mineral springs. Many believe that the waters cure or prevent ailments such as indigestion, eczema, and rheumatism.

Heaven Lake fills the crater atop Baektu Mountain, which straddles the border between China and North Korea.

ISLANDS

The Korean peninsula has many natural harbors on its southern and western coasts. There are beaches where streams enter the sea. The east has few beaches, because mountains line the coast.

More than 3,400 islands surround the Korean peninsula, mostly off the southern and southwestern coasts. Apart from the development of fisheries during the twentieth century, life for the islanders has remained relatively unchanged for centuries.

The grandfather stones, or stone grandfathers, are a symbol of Jeju Island.

Jeju Island, Korea's largest island, located approximately sixty miles (95 km) south of the peninsula, has a population of about 600,000. It is a popular vacation site, sometimes called "the Hawaii of South Korea," with its palm trees, spectacular beaches, caves, casinos, and golf courses. Tourism is one of the island's biggest sources of income; in 2013, more than ten million tourists visited Jeju, about 70 percent of them from the Korean mainland.

A popular attraction are the grandfather stones (*dolharubang*)—large statues reminiscent of the maoi of Easter Island. The massive statues were built around 1750 to frighten off invaders. In addition, three Jeju Volcanic Island and Lava Tubes parks make up an official World Heritage Site, as determined by the United Nations Educational, Scientific and Cultural Organization (UNESCO).

Due to its isolation in times past, the language and culture of Jeju are quite different from that of mainland Korea, and its residents live in a matriarchal, or female-dominated, society.

CLIMATE

The Korean peninsula has a temperate climate and experiences four seasons each year. Monsoon rains make summer hot and wet, while winter is cold and dry. During summer, from mid-June to mid-September, heavy monsoon

A beautiful landscape beckons at a park in Seoraksan National Park.

rains account for nearly 70 percent of the peninsula's annual rainfall. In South Korea, summer temperatures range between 75°F and 85°F (24°C and 29°C). This kind of weather supports rice cultivation.

In the north, summers are cooler: the average temperature is 68°F (20°C). The north also receives less rain annually, between 24 and 40 inches (60 and 100 cm), than the 40 to 55 inches (100 to 140 cm) that the south receives.

The fall, from mid-September to mid-November, is Korea's shortest season. Frost first appears on October nights. Days are often pleasantly clear and crisp, with temperatures ranging from 55°F to 65°F (13°C to 18°C). The dry weather enables rice crops to ripen and be harvested. Winter crops such as wheat and barley are planted during the fall.

Winter, from mid-November to March, is not as severe in the south as in the north. Snow accounts for only 5 to 10 percent of the annual precipitation in South Korea, and rice and barley can be grown during winter. The north experiences bitter winters, with temperatures that range from 21°F to -8°F (-6°C to -22°C), the lower extreme being typical of the northern interior.

Spring, from April to mid-June, is short, when the snow thaws and rainfall increases.

FLORA

Korea's climate and terrain sustain large forests with a variety of trees. However, sections of the woodlands have disappeared. Chemicals used during the Korean War (1950—1953) caused defoliation; torrential rains have caused erosion; and demand for fuel and timber have caused deforestation. Major reforestation efforts have been implemented since the late 1960s. Tree species that will contribute to future timber needs are generally selected for planting.

Varieties of pine, maple, oak, poplar, birch, and willow are common in Korea. Fir, spruce, larch, and Korean cedar are abundant in the northern mountains. Reeds and sedges grow in stony lowlands that flood easily. The leaves of the rush plant, which grows in marshy areas, are woven into mats and baskets. There are also many endemic herbs, and herbal medicine is widely practiced.

Korea's flowering plants include camellia, forsythia, lilac, chrysanthemum, azalea, and rose. Azaleas, which are often depicted in Korean painting and poetry, color the hills bright pink in early spring. The national flower, the *mugunghwa*, or "Rose of Sharon," is a hardy hibiscus that reblooms after a flower is cut. The plant has a long growing season and symbolizes Korea's strength in adversity.

Fruit trees also flourish in South Korea. Apples, pears, peaches, tangerines, persimmons, figs, and cherries are abundant. Native nuts include pine nuts, chestnuts, walnuts, and gingko nuts. In the warmer, subtropical climate of Jeju, bananas and pineapples are grown.

The sturdy Rose of Sharon, or mugunghwa, is a symbol of South Korea.

FAUNA

Animals found in Korea include badgers, bears, deer, leopards, weasels, wildcats, wolves, smaller mammals such as shrews, muskrats, and the Jindo dog, from the island of Jin, off the southwestern coast.

More than 350 bird species have been recorded on the Korean Peninsula. Cranes, crows, herons, magpies, orioles, robins, and swallows are widespread, while migratory ducks, teals, swans, and geese arrive or pass through during certain times of year.

The crane, often depicted in traditional Korean painting, is considered a symbol of good luck. The black-and-white magpie is a welcome sight early in the morning, as it is thought to bring good news.

A KOREAN TREASURE

Constructed in the fifteenth century during the Joseon Dynasty, the Changdeokgung Palace sits at the foot of Mount Baegaksan in the northern part of Seoul. The extensive complex of official and royal residential buildings and gardens covers 143 acres (58 ha).

The site was designed according to pungsu *and Confucian principals. (Pungsu is a type of Korean feng shui, a philosophy of topography, line, and pattern and how they relate to human life.) The palace buildings, therefore, were designed to fit in to their natural surroundings in a harmonious way.*

The palace was used as a residence by Korean emperors until 1896. Today it is a tourist attraction, the highlight for many visitors being the beautiful and serene Secret Garden. The design of the estate had a great influence on the development of Korean architecture, garden design, and landscape planning, as well as other art forms for many centuries. It is one of South Korea's eleven UNESCO World Heritage Sites.

CITIES

South Korea's most populous cities are Seoul (eleven million), Busan (four million), Daegu (2.6 million), and Incheon (2.5 million).

SEOUL This metropolis on the Han River ranks as one of the ten largest cities in the world. South Korea's capital serves as its political, economic, educational, and cultural hub. The city has been the capital since the Joseon dynasty, more than five hundred years ago. Not far from the ultramodern hotels in the heart of Seoul are the ancient palaces. A ten-mile (16-km) wall was built around the city hundreds of years ago. There were nine gates in the wall, providing access into the city. Four of the gates were destroyed over the years.

BUSAN Busan is South Korea's largest port, its second-largest city, and the center of its fishing industry. With about four million inhabitants, Busan has tremendous industrial activity. Yet it remains one of Korea's most popular resort cities, with its historical landmarks, beautiful beaches, and hot mineral springs.

DAEGU South Korea's third-largest city is a major industrial hub, the nation's largest textile producer. Daegu is also a center for education. There are five colleges and four universities in the city.

Daegu is home to the Dalseong Fortress, built more than 1,700 years ago and now preserved in Dalseong Park. Daegu was once known as a market city specializing in apples and medicinal herbs. The city has adopted the eagle, magnolia, and fir tree as its symbols.

The stream flows away endlessly/ And the waterfall plummets down from the sky/ These remind me of a white rainbow, thunder and light flooding the valleys.
–a poem by King Sukjong (reigned 1674-1720), carved in Chinese characters into a rock in the Secret Garden at the Changdeokgung Palace

The city of Busan sits at the foot of Geumjeong Mountain on the southeastern coast of the Korean Peninsula.

THE DEMILITARIZED ZONE

During the Korean War (1950–1953), the farming village of Panmunjom was obliterated. Today the location of the abandoned village lies within the Demilitarized Zone, or DMZ, that divides the Korean Peninsula roughly in half and serves as a buffer zone separating North Korea and South Korea.

The DMZ is 2.5 miles (4 km) wide and stretches 152 miles (245 km) from the East Sea to the Yellow Sea. Despite its name, it is one of the most heavily militarized borders in the world. The Military Demarcation Line (MDL) runs through the center of the DMZ and indicates exactly where the war front was when the agreement was signed. Soldiers from both sides patrol the DMZ but may not cross the MDL. Over the years, there have been a number of skirmishes and incidents between the sides, but curiously, tourists are allowed to visit this dangerous area. Panmunjom today is the location of the Joint Security Area (JSA), the place where reunification and other talks between the two Koreas occasionally take place.

For the most part, no people are allowed elsewhere in the DMZ. This has had the unintended consequence of creating a de facto nature preserve for many plants and animals, including several endangered species, within this human-free buffer zone.

INCHEON Located west of Seoul, Incheon is home to an international airport. With its beautiful beaches, the port city is popular among vacationers during summer. Incheon has a tidal range of sixty feet (18 m)—the second highest in the world. Nearby is Korea's fifth-largest island, Ganghwa, known for its historical sites.

The entrance to the Heavenly Horse Tomb in Tumuli Park leads to a chamber that was excavated in 1973. The tomb was probably that of an unknown king of Silla Kingdom, dating to the fifth or sixth century CE.

GYEONGJU This ancient city, the site of kings' tombs, pagodas, and Buddhist temples, is Korea's museum-without-walls. Gyeongju was the capital of the Silla dynasty, which flourished from 57 BCE to 935 CE.

In 1973 archeologists unearthed 11,500 artifacts from a Silla burial chamber, now called the Heavenly Horse Tomb. The thousands of historical treasures found in the Gyeongju Valley have prompted the United Nations Education, Scientific, and Cultural Organization (UNESCO) to name the city one of the world's ten most important ancient cities.

INTERNET LINKS

english.visitkorea.or.kr
"Imagine Your Korea," a site sponsored by the Korean Tourism, has information and photo galleries.

ngm.nationalgeographic.com/features/world/asia/north-korea/dmz-text/1
This *National Geographic* article "Korea's DMZ: Dangerous Divide," is a fascinating, up-close look at the DMZ.

whc.unesco.org/en/list/816
This is the UNESCO World Heritage page for the Changdeokgung Palace Complex.

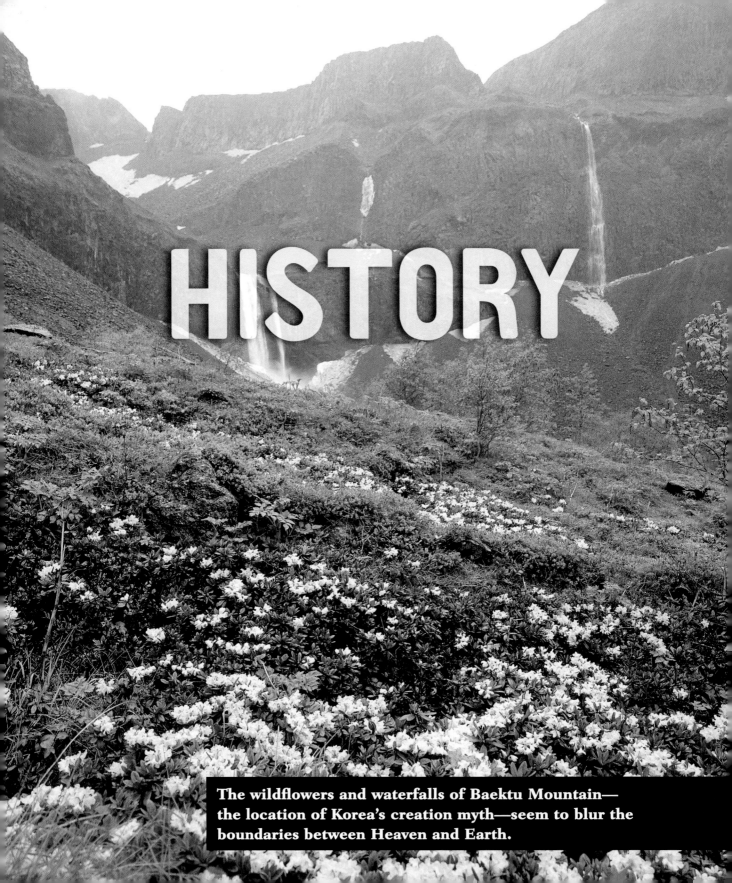

HISTORY

The wildflowers and waterfalls of Baektu Mountain—
the location of Korea's creation myth—seem to blur the
boundaries between Heaven and Earth.

2

I N THE BEGINNING, THE LORD OF Heaven sent his son Hwanung to Earth to live on Baektu Mountain, a volcano on the border of China and Korea. From there, Hwanung conveyed great knowledge to the human beings.

A tiger and a bear asked Hwanung if he would make them human. He agreed, but only if they could first endure one hundred days in a cave eating nothing but garlic and mugwort. The steadfast bear endured and became a beautiful woman. Hwanung took the bear-woman as his wife and she gave birth to Dangun, the legendary father of Korea. But the tiger grew hungry and impatient. He left the cave after only twenty days, and has been wandering the Korean mountains ever since.

Historically, Dangun established the first kingdom, Gojoseon, in 2333 BCE. The Dangun era, also known as Ancient Joseon, lasted more than one thousand years. On October 3 each year, South Korea celebrates Dangun Day, also known as National Foundation Day.

Legend aside, archaeologists have determined that some prehistoric people probably migrated to the Korean Peninsula from Siberia, Manchuria, and Mongolia. These early people were hunters, fishermen, and farmers who practiced shamanism and worshipped spirits of nature. Their system of beliefs has survived in Korea through five millennia.

THE ANCIENT KOREANS

Neolithic (late Stone Age) peoples who entered the Korean peninsula possibly as early as 6,000 BCE drove out the Paleolithic (early Stone Age)

North Korea and South Korea have different versions of the peninsula's history. Each version differs in detail and perspective, reflecting the influences of China, Russia, Japan, and the United States; the aggressor in one version may be the victim in the other.

Cheomseongdae, in Gyeongju, is the oldest existing astronomical observatory in Asia and dates to the Silla Kingdom. It is one of South Korea's National Treasures.

peoples who were already living there. It is believed that the new settlers were the ancestors of modern-day Koreans.

The cultural development of the early Koreans was influenced by developments in China. Chinese models of civilization shaped Korean society. In 108 BCE the Chinese had a more direct impact when the Han dynasty established four territories in the northern half of the Korean peninsula. That event began Korea's recorded history.

In 75 BCE the Koreans recaptured three of the four territories. The remaining territory, Lalang, remained under Chinese control. It was through the flourishing Chinese colony of Lalang that characteristics of Chinese civilization—such as the system of writing, ideas on religion, government systems, and the art of iron working—were transmitted to the Koreans.

THREE KINGDOMS

By the first century CE, there were three Korean kingdoms. Silla was founded in 57 BCE, Goguryeo in 37 BCE, and Baekje in 18 BCE. The kingdom of Goguryeo, geographically the closest to China, was formed when several peoples united in the northeastern region of the peninsula. Initially the most powerful of the three kingdoms, Goguryeo established its capital where Pyongyang, the capital of North Korea, now stands.

The kingdom of Baekje was founded by peoples who migrated southward to avoid the aggression of warriors from Goguryeo. Eventually these peoples occupied southern Korea, establishing their capital near Seoul.

Silla, the richest and most cultured of the three kingdoms, established its capital at Gyeongju. In 618 CE the Tang dynasty came to power in China. Its rulers were eager to expand their sphere of influence. Capitalizing on hostilities among the three Korean kingdoms, the Tang dynasty helped Silla gain control over the peninsula, hoping to eventually control the expanded Silla. Silla conquered Baekje in 660 and Goguryeo in 668, but then encouraged revolts in Baekje and Goguryeo and defeated the Chinese troops that were sent to quell the revolts. Eventually, China agreed to recognize Silla as an independent state.

Silla spread its cultural influence throughout the peninsula, which was finally united under one Korean government.

UNIFIED SILLA (668—935 CE) The Unified Silla period is often referred to as Korea's golden age of art and culture. Beautiful temples and shrines were built. The complicated Chinese writing system used in Korea was simplified, encouraging the spread of literature. Other forms of the arts also flourished, and Korea became a great center for architecture, painting, music, and crafts such as ceramics, lacquerware, ironware, and gold and silver jewelry.

Artifacts that have been discovered among the remains of temples, tombs, and pagodas in Gyeongju, the capital of Unified Silla, reveal the remarkable accomplishments of the period. Some of these were the development of irrigation systems that improved rice cultivation, land reforms that benefited the poor, and the establishment of a national university. The economy boomed, as trade between East Asian nations expanded.

Unified Silla started to decline around 780 when infighting began among nobles. After many violent clashes, Wang Kon, the leader of a separatist faction, conquered Goguryeo, then Baekje, and finally Silla. In 918 he proclaimed himself the leader of a new state, with its capital at Songdo (present-day Kaesong). Wang Kon called his nation *Goryeo*, a shortened form of the name Goguryeo, from which the name of Korea was later derived. A capable leader, Wang Kon was renamed *Daejo*, which means "first king," after his death.

This map shows the Three Kingdoms of ancient Korea.

The Mausoleum of Wang Kon stands in Kaesong, which was the capital of Goryeo.

GORYEO (918—1392) Korean culture thrived during the eleventh century. Buddhism flourished through Goryeo patronage and became a powerful force in politics and culture. Buddhist scholars produced writings and art, and numerous temples and pagodas were built. Artists of the time also made valuable celadon pottery and devised a form of poetry known as *sijo* (SAE-jo).

In the later Goryeo period, Confucianism grew in influence. The aristocrats professed Buddhism but looked to Confucianism for political and ethical guidance. Schools teaching Confucianism were built next to Buddhist temples.

In 1231, the Mongols invaded Goryeo. But by then, the Goryeo kingdom had problems. Aristocrats owned most of the land, and some tenant farmers resorted to selling themselves as servants to pay the heavy taxes. Dissatisfied with the former Buddhist leaders, the government had recruited a team of neo-Confucian scholar-officials. It could not pay the new leaders well enough though, and they became disillusioned.

A new leader arose to meet the challenges facing the government. General Yi Seong-gye took over leadership of the kingdom in a peaceful coup in 1392 and founded the Joseon dynasty.

JOSEON (1392—1910) General Yi realized that reforms were necessary if his reign was to be successful. He restructured the government and based it on Confucian concepts, emphasizing respect for elders and ancestors. Books on Confucian classics and literature were printed to encourage higher learning. Some of the ceremonies introduced in the dynasty are still practiced in Korea today.

Under Yi's rule, land was redistributed and Buddhist temples closed. The capital was moved to Hanyang (present-day Seoul), where Yi's dynasty, consisting of a small group of nobles, stayed for more than five hundred years. Like Wang Kon, Yi was given the title Daejo after his death.

Sejong, the fourth ruler of the Joseon dynasty, showed tremendous concern for Confucian ethics.

A statue of Sejong the Great was erected in Gwanghamun Square in Seoul in 2009.

Class distinctions were firmly established during his reign in an attempt to create an ideal Confucian state. The importance of proper conduct between the individual and the family, and between the individual and the state were especially emphasized. Sejong was considered the greatest Joseon king. His rule saw developments in technology, science, philosophy, and music. A major achievement was the creation of *hangeul* (HAHN-gool), a phonetic alphabet that could be used by the masses because of its simplicity.

Soon after Sejong's reign, the country fell under siege again. The Mongols presented a persistent threat at the border, and the Japanese raided the coast relentlessly.

THE IMJIN WAR

In 1592, Japan waged war on Korea. Under the powerful military leader Toyotomi Hideyoshi, who desired to rule all of Asia, Japan invaded Korea and conquered the cities of Busan, Seoul, and, in the north, Pyongyang.

A re-creation of a turtleboat, or turtle ship, stands at the War Memorial in Seoul.

In 1598, after six devastating years of war, the Koreans finally forced the Japanese out with help from China. Were it not for the brilliance of Admiral Yi Sunsin, the inventor of an ironclad ship called a turtleboat, Korea's efforts might have failed. Farmland had been destroyed, and artisans and technicians captured and brought to Japan. The ravages of war and the loss of some of its finest minds left Korea a weak and unproductive state.

In the early 1600s, faced with Chinese aggression, Korea paid large amounts of money to avoid war. After its unfortunate encounters with foreign powers, Korea isolated itself from all nations except China, and became known as the Hermit Kingdom. But in doing so, Korean society stagnated while other nations experienced a rich period of intellectual achievement.

China kept its stranglehold on Korea until Japan defeated China in the Sino-Japanese War (1894—95). Then in 1904, Russia fought Japan for Korea in the Russo-Japanese War, which Japan won in 1905. That victory resulted in the Japanese annexation of Korea in 1910; and Japan stripped Korea of its rights as an independent nation. A new, highly oppressive era began.

JAPANESE RULE

After Japan annexed Korea in 1910, Japanese citizens, helped by the new government, took over Korean businesses and landholdings. The Japanese exploited Korea's natural resources and built roads, railroads, ports, and dams, thus modernizing Korea.

However, Korean culture suffered. Koreans were forced to adopt Japanese names and to participate in Japanese religious rituals. The Korean language was prohibited from being taught to or even spoken by Korean students in schools.

Japan's oppressive rule motivated the historically complacent Korean people to stage demonstrations to gain international support for Korean independence. Major protests were held throughout the country in a united effort after the Korean delegation at the post-World War I Versailles Conference near Paris failed to gain approval for self-rule in 1919.

Japanese forces moved to quell the independence movement, called *Samil*, or the March First Movement. The pro-independence groups held more than 1500 protest rallies with the participation of more than two million civilians. During these protests, some 7,500 people were killed and 46,000 were arrested. Despite the campaign's failure to achieve its goal of independence, March 1 is celebrated as a national holiday in both North and South Korea today.

KOREA DIVIDED

When the Allies (the United States, Great Britain, France, and fourteen other nations) defeated the Japanese in World War II, the Korean peninsula's fate fell into different hands. Caught in the Cold War, the United States and the Soviet Union worked to prevent each other from taking control of Korea.

The Soviet Union pushed for a communist government, while the United States insisted on a capitalist system. The two nations agreed that the Soviet Union would accept the Japanese surrender north of the 38th parallel, while

Transport vehicles of the U.N. force withdraw from North Korea, crossing the famous 38th Parallel, during the Korean War.

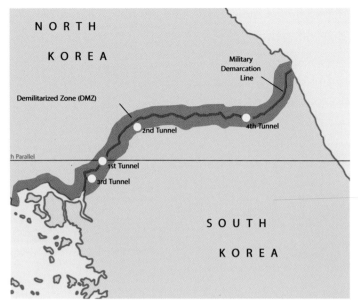

The map shows the area of the Demilitarized Zone, which crosses the 38th Parallel. It also marks the locations of secret tunnels constructed by North Korea for use in transporting troops and equipment into the South surreptitiously.

American troops would stay south of the line until a plan was developed to reunite Korea. When, after two years, the two nations still could not reach an agreement on Korea's future, the United States turned the situation over to the United Nations.

The United Nations' solution was to give the Koreans the power to decide on the issue in a free election. But since the Soviet Union would not allow the U.N. Commission that was to oversee the election into the north of the peninsula, an election was held only in the southern half in 1948. Syngman Rhee won the presidency, the Republic of Korea was formed, and its National Assembly drew up a constitution. Shortly after, the Soviet Union announced the formation of the Democratic People's Republic of Korea, led by a communist general, Kim Il Sung. Both governments claimed to represent the whole country.

THE KOREAN WAR

In June 1950 North Korean armed forces attacked South Korea in an attempt to unify the peninsula. The event marked the beginning of the Korean War. South Korea was caught off guard and the North rapidly advanced.

American soldiers entered the war in September but were forced to retreat to the southeastern corner. Subsequently a U.N. force consisting of combatants from sixteen nations was sent to support South Korea, but even so, 88 percent of the combined force were U.S. soldiers. When the U.N. force moved into North Korea close to the Chinese border, China entered the conflict in support of the communists. Although no Soviet troops participated, the Soviet Union provided tactical support to North Korea.

A stalemate resulted, with armies positioned at the middle of the Korean Peninsula. The Korean Armistice Agreement, signed in July 1953 by representatives of the military forces on both sides, arranged for a ceasefire, the establishment of the Demilitarized Zone, and the means of dealing with the prisoners of war.

However, since the armistice is a an agreement between military forces and not between the governments of North Korea and South Korea, it is not a peace treaty. Since 1953, no peace treaty has been signed, which means the Korean War has not officially ended. Although the armistice is still officially in effect, North Korea has announced on several occasions that it is no longer abiding by the agreement. However, the U.N.'s position is that since the armistice was adopted by the U.N. General Assembly, neither North Korea nor South Korea can dissolve it independently.

The war dealt a heavy blow on both sides of the 38th Parallel. The war cost the lives of some five million Koreans and Chinese, as well as more than 50,000 Americans. The North Korean population was drastically reduced, and cropland throughout South Korea was ravaged and Seoul nearly leveled. Political differences keep the two Koreas apart. North Korea remains steadfastly communist, while South Korea is firmly capitalist. Yet, such opposing ideals have not crushed the hopes of the Korean people for eventual reunification.

"It was here on July 27, 1953 that the American imperialists got down on their knees before the heroic Chosun people to sign the ceasefire for the war they had provoked June 25, 1950." –inscription in the North Korean Peace Museum, which was the building in which the 1953 armistice was signed.

U.S. troops wait for the attack order as North Korean troops launch a great offensive into Seoul in April 1951.

NORTH KOREA: THE NEW HERMIT KINGDOM

On July 27, 2013, North Korean soldiers march through Kim Il-Sung Square in Pyongyang during a military parade marking the sixtieth anniversary of the Korean War armistice.

The Korean War never officially ended, especially not in the north. The war's presence is constantly felt in Democratic People's Republic of Korea (DPRK, or North Korea), which is often said to be one of the strangest, most oppressive nations on Earth. Despite its name, there is nothing democratic about it.

North Korea is a place where time and truth seem to exist in an alternative reality. (In fact, it's not the twenty-first century there, where the official calendar is the Juche calendar, adopted in 1996. It counts the years from the birth date of the nation's first leader, Kim Il-Sung, who was born in 1912. Therefore 1912 was Juche 1 and the years progress from there. The year 2014 was Juche 103 and so forth.)

The DPRK is a completely closed society. Although tourists are allowed into the country, their itineraries are controlled and they are supervised at all times to make sure they see only what the government wants them to see.

Communication of any sort between North Korean citizens and foreigners is forbidden, as is the Internet and any other source of information from outside the country. North Koreans are taught that their country is the happiest place on Earth and the envy of every nation.

MILITARY North Korea is about the size of Pennsylvania, yet has the fifth largest military in the world, as determined by the number of active personnel (more than a million). If reserve personnel are included (more than eight million), the Korean People's Army, as it is called, becomes the largest military organization in the world. With a "military-first" economic policy, North Korea spends about one-quarter of its money (gross domestic product, or GDP) supporting its army.

In 2005, children at a government-run nursery in Pyongyang eat food provided by the World Food Program.

Why does such a small country need such a large army? The North Korean people are taught that they live under the constant threat of invasion by the United States. South Korea, according to this view, has been occupied by the United States since the end of the Korean War, which the North Koreans are taught was started by a U.S. invasion. Constant fear keeps the people loyal to their leaders, whose protection is seen to be the only thing standing between them and certain annihilation. This permanent siege mentality accounts for the extreme militarism of every aspect of North Korean life.

HUNGER Meanwhile, many people in North Korea are starving. In 2013, the UN reported that 28 percent of North Korean children suffer from chronic malnutrition, which has stunted their growth. Two-thirds of the country's 24 million people are food-insecure, which means they don't know where their next meal is coming from. Even among those who have enough to eat, the diet is often nutritionally poor. The World Food Program in 2013 said about 80 percent of North Korean households lacked the essential amount of vitamins, minerals, fats, and proteins in their diets.

In 2010, Robert Park, a Korean-American human rights activist, decries the brutal treatment of inmates in secret North Korean prison camps.

LACK OF FREEDOM The DPRK ranked 178th—or dead last—in the world on the 2014 Index of Economic Freedom as determined by the Heritage Foundation. The index is an annual measurement of nations' economic freedom, prosperity, and opportunity. North Korea is lowest on the list under the category of "repressed." For comparison, South Korea is ranked 31, which places it in the category "mostly free."

The world has long known of secret prison camps in North Korea holding an estimated 150,000—200,000 political prisoners and others. People are not told the charges against them, and there are no trials. Entire extended families of political prisoners may be incarcerated for life—even grandparents, children, and babies—through three generations. Prisoners are deliberately kept on the brink of starvation and made to work hard physical labor. The mortality rate in these camps is very high, perhaps 40 percent. There are no official statistics because the government denies the prison camps even exist. (Satellite photos prove otherwise.)

KIM IL-SUNG (1912—1994) was the president of the Democratic People's Republic of Korea from its establishment in 1948 until his death. He created a "cult of personality" that continues to this day.

A cult of personality is a political and social phenomenon in which a living person, usually a leader or authority figure, is idolized and revered as perfect or godlike. Such a situation is often a trait of totalitarian regimes—those in which the government has total power—which is certainly the case in North Korea. Government-sponsored propaganda deliberately and relentlessly promotes the illusion of a heroic, superhuman leader—one who is not only beyond criticism, but literally the source of all life, security, and happiness in the nation.

Kim developed the ideology of Juche, a central component of the North Korean way of thinking. It promotes a North Korean style of nationalistic socialism that exalts political independence, economic self sufficiency, and personal self-reliance.

Huge portraits of North Korean leaders Kim Il-Sung and his son Kim Jong-Il dominate Kim Il-Sung Square in Pyongyang.

Today Kim is affectionately referred to as the "Great Leader," and the "Eternal President." Enormous statues and posters of him are almost everywhere across the country.

KIM JONG-IL (1941—2011) was the son of Kim Il-Sung and was North Korea's Supreme Leader from 1994 until his death. He continued the cult of personality inherited from his father, and became a new focus for the people's worship. Many Koreans believed the "Dear Leader" had supernatural powers, and could, for example, control the weather with his moods.

During his rule, North Korea secretly developed nuclear weapons in direct opposition to the 1994 Agreed Framework it negotiated with the United States. A severe famine from 1994—1998 devastated the populace, killing hundreds of thousands, and perhaps millions, of North Koreans. International observers accused the Kim government of "crimes against humanity" for creating policies that produced and prolonged the starvation. In 2002, U.S. President George W. Bush famously portrayed North Korea as one of three countries (the other two were Iraq and Iran) that formed an "Axis of Evil." And in 2004, Human Rights Watch reported that North Korea under Kim was "among the world's most repressive governments."

Kim Jong-Il initiated the national policy of *Songun*, or "military first," that directs the nation's wealth and assets to the support of the military above all.

After his death in 2011, Kim Jong-Il's preserved body was placed on permanent public display, as is his father's, at the Kumsusan Memorial Palace in Pyongyang.

North Korean middle school students use hand hoes to cultivate a hillside south of Pyongyang. They planted trees as well as beans and peanuts.

KIM JONG-UN (b. 1983) Kim Jong-Il's youngest son, became the Supreme Leader in 2011. At the time, the international community wondered if the new Kim might signal a change in leadership, and an easing of the extreme oppression of North Korean rule, but those hopes were soon dashed. Kim Jong-Un avidly took to playing his role in the cult of personality and, for a time, threatened "preemptive" war against South Korea and nuclear attacks on the United States. In addition, he is thought to have ordered the executions of numerous political figures.

In 2012, Kim Jong-Un salutes the troops as he watches a military parade.

INTERNET LINKS

www.pbs.org/hiddenkorea/history.htm
PBS, "Hidden Korea" is an introduction to Korea's history and culture.

www.britannica.com/EBchecked/topic/364173/March-First-Movement
Encyclopaedia Brittanica, "March First Movement" explains Korean resistance to Japanese occupation.

www.pbs.org/wgbh/pages/frontline/shows/kim
PBS, "Kim's Nuclear Gamble" is the website for the Frontline TV show that examined North Korea's nuclear capacity.

www.history.com/topics/korean-war
History.com's "The Korean War" has articles, videos, photos, and speeches.

GOVERNMENT

South Korean President-elect Park Geun-Hye celebrates with her party members after she is declared the winner of the presidential elections on December 19, 2012 in Seoul.

3

I N FEBRUARY 2013, PARK GEUN-HYE became the eighteenth president of the Republic of Korea (ROK). She is the first female president since the establishment of the South Korean government. Her father was President Park Chung-hee, who served from 1963—1979.

Since its establishment in 1948, the Republic of Korea has had universal suffrage, meaning all eligible citizens can vote. As of 2014, the voting age in South Korea was nineteen. In 2005, it was lowered from the previous

South Koreans cast their votes in provincial elections held nationwide in June 2014.

"My father was criticized as a dictator, but that should not overshadow his accomplishments in restructuring the country. He brought Korea out of five thousand years of poverty. What he left unaccomplished was democratization of the system."
—Park Geun-hye, President of South Korea, assumed office in 2013

age of twenty. Voter participation in elections has been falling in recent years, and some advocates are trying to push the government to lower the age of eligibility to eighteen in order to get interest young people in the democratic process.

THE CONSTITUTION

South Korea's constitution was adopted in 1948 and has since been revised nine times. The constitution allows for three branches of government: the executive, headed by the president; the National Assembly; and the judiciary. The South Korean president is elected for a single five-year term. He or she can appoint or dismiss the prime minister, with the National Assembly's approval, as well as ministers and heads of office. The president is both head of foreign relations and commander-in-chief of the armed forces.

THE NATIONAL ASSEMBLY

The National Assembly is South Korea's lawmaking body. Voters elect two-thirds of the members of the assembly for four-year terms. The remaining third are represented proportionately by political parties winning five or more seats in the election. Some of the functions of the assembly are: to propose, pass, or reject legislative bills; to ratify foreign treaties; to confirm or reject the appointment of the prime minister; and to oversee administrative agencies.

THE ARMED FORCES

South Korea's military consists of the army, navy, air force, Marine Corp, and Coast Guard. In 2012, the force consisted of 3,539,000, with 639,000 active

members and 2,900,000 in reserve. Military service is compulsory for men ages eighteen to twenty-eight for up to twenty-six months. South Korea has the twelfth highest defense budget in the world, with a budget of more than $30 billion. South Korea's armed forces exist mainly to contain aggression by the North, but they also participate in various peacekeeping missions around the world.

South Korean soldiers participate in an anti-chemical, anti-biological terror drill in 2013 in Seoul.

SOUTH KOREA'S ROAD TO DEMOCRACY

The ROK's first president, Syngman Rhee, promised to introduce democracy in the nation. But his dictatorial style and corrupt leadership led to nationwide student protests, forcing him to step down in 1960.

In 1961 General Park Chung Hee proclaimed martial law. He later retired from the military and won the 1963 presidential election. Under Park's leadership, the constitution was amended to increase presidential power; freedom of speech and of the press were severely restricted. Although he

The Blue House is South Korea's White House. That is, the Cheongwadae, *(literally "pavilion of blue tiles") is the official residence and executive office building of the ROK's president. Built in traditional Korean architectural style, the Blue House is actually a*

relatively new building, with the main residence completed in 1991. It is roofed in blue tiles in a distinctively Korean hue, and is one of numerous official buildings situated on beautiful park-like grounds in Seoul.

Just as the term "White House" is used to indicate the U.S. presidency, the term "Blue House" is used in a similar fashion in reference to the ROK head of state.

oversaw tremendous growth and modernization of the ROK's economy—a phenomenon often called the "Miracle on the Han River," and modernization of the country in general, many people accused Park of being a dictator. After surviving several assassination attempts, including two that involved North Korea, Park was assassinated in 1979 by Kim Jae-kyu, the director of the Korean Central Intelligence Service and the president's security chief, for reasons that remain unclear.

The military then took over the government. Attempts to restore constitutional rights led to violent clashes between the military and demonstrators. In 1980 General Chun Doo Hwan, who led the military action against the demonstrators, took control of the nation. His presidency was marked by student demonstrations for the reinstatement of direct elections.

In 1987 Roh Tae Woo, a former general, won the presidency. Because he had been a major participant in the 1979 coup, many questioned his commitment to democracy. In 1992 Roh was replaced by Kim Young Sam.

Kim introduced political and economic reforms, but his term was plagued by corruption. In 1998 Kim Young Sam was succeeded by Kim Dae Jung.

Kim Dae Jung was branded a communist by Park for his liberal views on reunification, but he remained popular among the people. In his first presidential race, Kim won 46 percent of the votes, but lost to Park. He continued his campaign against Park despite political persecution. In 1973 he was taken from his hotel in Tokyo by South Korean agents and held prisoner for days. He was released only when the U.S. ambassador intervened.

When Park was assassinated in 1979, the new president, Chun, imposed martial law and arrested Kim and other opposition leaders. The United States intervened, and Kim left for the United States in 1982. When he returned to Korea several years later, he was put under house arrest. Kim persevered through another two electoral losses before winning in 1997, at the height of the Asian economic crisis and at the age of seventy-two. He was openly opposed to authoritarian rule and initiated a "Sunshine Policy" of engagement

South Korean President Kim Dae-Jung joins hands with North Korean leader Kim Jong-Il before signing an agreement between the two countries in June 2000.

The Taegeukgi *is the flag of the Republic of Korea. Its design symbolizes certain principles Chinese philosophy. The circle in the center of the flag is a* taeguk, *also known as the yin-yang symbol. It represents the interconnected duality of the* yin *and the* yang, *the complementary cosmic forces that rule the natural world. The upper red section represents the positive forces of the yang. The lower blue section represents the negative, or opposite, forces of the yin. The two forces together embody the balance and harmony of the universe. The circle is surrounded by four trigrams, one in each corner. Each trigram symbolizes one of the four universal elements: heaven (☰), earth (☷), fire (☲), and water (☵).*

and cooperation with the North. In 2000 Kim was awarded the Nobel Peace Prize for his efforts, though his accomplishment was later tarnished by allegations of bribery to North Korea. Kim died in 2009, and in 2010, the ROK government declared the Sunshine Policy a failure and discontinued it. Nevertheless, Kim's presidency helped push South Korea further along the road to becoming a strong democracy.

POLITICAL PARTIES

As of 2014, the ruling party in South Korea is the Saenuri Party ("New Frontier Party") of President Park Geun-hye. It is a conservative party formerly called the Grand National Party. Conservatism in South Korea is fervently anti-communist and opposes relations with North Korea. It favors domestic modernization and social stability.

The main opposition party is the New Politics Alliance for Democracy, a liberal democratic party. "Liberal" in South Korea has a different meaning

than it does in U.S. politics, and is characterized by patriotism and ethnic nationalism, and as such, tends to favor engagement with the North. Former liberal leaders were presidents Kim Dae-jung and Roh Moo-hyun.

Seoul mayor-elect Park Won-Soon of the New Politics Alliance for Democracy Party celebrates his electoral victory with his supporters in June 2014.

INTERNET LINKS

english.president.go.kr
The official site of the Republic of Korea's president, which also includes information about the Blue House.

infographics.idlelist.com/the-meaning-of-taegukgi-the-south-korean-flag
A graphic explanation of the symbolism of the ROK flag.

ECONOMY

Morning commuters walk along a train platform at
Seoul Station.

4

I N THE IMMEDIATE AFTERMATH OF THE Korean War, South Korea had a poor, mostly agricultural economy, one that was comparable to the poorer countries in Africa and Asia. Before 1960 there were few developed industries. The division of the peninsula into two independent states disrupted domestic trade patterns and left South Korea without access to the mineral resources in the North. However, since then, South Korea's economy has grown tremendously. It is now a major global producer of steel, iron, automobiles, ships, and electronics.

Today, as one of the world's wealthiest nations, South Korea is one of the G-20, or Group of Twenty major world economies. Korea is also a member of the Organization for Economic Co-operation and Development (OECD), an international economic organization of thirty-four countries committed to democracy and the market economy. In fact, Korea's gross domestic production (GDP), a measure used to determine a country's economic strength, of $1.32 trillion (in 2014) put it among the top twelve economies in the world.

"In human life, economics precedes politics or culture."
—South Korea's president Park Chung-hee

The key to the turnaround were government policies instituted by President Park Chung Hee. They promoted the importation of raw materials that were lacking on the peninsula and placed a new emphasis on savings and investment over consumption.

South Korea is one of the few countries in the world that avoided a recession after the global financial crisis in 2008. It has had steady economic growth since that time. The growth rate for 2014 was estimated to be 4 percent in contrast to the United States which has had a growth rate of 1.5 percent during the same period.

A worker labels a stack of aluminum ingots at the Public Procurement Service warehouse in Gunsan.

INDUSTRIES IN SOUTH KOREA

MANUFACTURING   Although nearly all of South Korea's industries are privately owned, there is often cooperation between the government and the private sector. Sometimes the government develops new industries and slowly privatizes them; other times it offers incentives to entrepreneurs to start new businesses. This cooperation between private business and the government has led to the rise of huge business groups, known in Korea as *chaebol* (JAE-bull) or "conglomerates."

One well-known chaebol is Hyundai, which was founded in 1967. Today, Hyundai is made up of more than sixty subsidiary companies. It is active in a wide range of production including automobile manufacturing, construction, chemicals, electronics, financial services, heavy industry, and shipbuilding. Hyundai and South Korea's three other large chaebol—Lucky Goldstar (LG), SK, and Samsung—account for more than half of the nation's production.

In the last four decades, production of electronic goods such as television sets and computer chips has developed so significantly that South Korea is now a world leader in this sector. Machinery and ship building also play a major role in the industrial manufacturing of South Korea.

MINING Much of the mineral deposits on the Korean Peninsula are located in North Korea and are thus unavailable for manufacturing. Limited quantities of coal, gold, silver, tungsten, talc, and iron ore are mined in the south. With few natural resources, the nation is developing overseas mining interests to meet its needs.

CONSTRUCTION Construction has been an important South Korean export industry since the early 1960s and remains a critical source of foreign currency and export earnings. South Korean construction workers are also active in building projects abroad, particularly in Southeast Asia, the Middle East, Latin America, and Africa.

Within the country, the flourishing economy has created a construction boom. Roads, buildings, and sewer systems are being developed to keep pace with economic growth.

SHIPBUILDING Korea and China dominate the shipbuilding industry worldwide. By the 1980s, Hyundai was building a large share of the world's oil

Workers construct an engine for a Hyundai vehicle on an assembly line at a factory in Asan.

The Seoul skyline at sunset, looking toward the Yeouido business district

Tourism is an important part of the South Korean economy. In 2013, some 12,175,550 people visited South Korea, and 14,846,485 Koreans left home to visit other parts of the world.

Being a mountainous country, South Korea offers tourists many vacation destinations of scenic beauty, including the Jungwon Valley, near Yongmunsan Mountain, with its streams and waterfalls.

Yongchu Valley in Gapyeong-gun and the Bigeum Valley in the Sudong National Tourist Park are also popular vacation places for Koreans as well as for visiting tourists.

The cities also offer a wealth of cultural attractions, including the temples, shrines, palaces, and folk villages of the UNESCO World Heritage sites. Seoul, the nation's capital, is a mix of ancient, traditional, and modern culture, and is the principal destination for international visitors.

Perhaps the top tourist destination in this country, however, is Jeju Island, off the southern tip of the Korean Peninsula. Also known as the "Island of the Gods," it has been compared to Hawaii, and is a popular honeymoon destination for Korean newlyweds.

A coastline on Jeju Island features unusual rock formations of basalt columnar joints.

supertankers, container ships and oil drilling platforms. Daewoo also became a major ship builder and by the 1990s, South Korea became the world's dominant shipbuilder with 50.8 percent of the world's shipbuilding market.

AUTOMOBILES Automobile manufacturing became one of South Korea's leading export industries by the 1990s. Today, South Korea is the world's fifth largest producer of automobiles. Hyundai Kia Automotive Group is Korea's largest automaker, and the second-largest automaker in Asia, after Japan's Toyota. In 2013, Hyundai-Kia ranked as the fifth largest automaker in the world, manufacturing some 7.5 million new cars and trucks.

AGRICULTURE AND FISHING

In the 1950s, agriculture represented about 70 percent of employment in South Korea. Today, a mere 9.5 percent of the workforce works in agriculture. Despite the drastic drop, there are still some 2 million small farms, most of which are privately owned rice farms. Rice is the most important crop in South Korea. Other South Korean crops include vegetables, soybeans, barley, and wheat. Livestock farming is also important, and pork, beef, and milk are the next three most important agricultural products after rice.

Traditional houses and rice fields make for a peaceful scene at Hahoe Folk Village, a preserved village from the Joseon Dynasty.

A worker at an electronics components factory in Suwon

Koreans have a strong work ethic. An average Korean works 2,316 hours per year, the longest of OECD Organisation for Economic Co-operation and Development (OECD) members where the average is 1,794 hours. The average Korean in a manufacturing job works up to fifty-five hours a week, compared to the forty-hour week of the average factory worker in the United States.

Korean society is based on a deeply rooted hierarchical social system. Koreans' respect for superiors takes the form of polite observances, such as rising in their presence and not leaving the workplace before them.

The polite and gentle demeanor of Koreans in social interactions is different from the competitiveness and tough negotiation skills they demonstrate in business. Koreans also have a deep-rooted loyalty. A Korean would give a job to someone whose loyalty he or she values rather than a person who may seem more capable.

FISHING South Korea is one of the world's leading fishing nations, with a fleet of more than 359 deep-sea vessels. Fish is a major export commodity and is the main source of protein in the Korean diet. In addition to the deep-sea fleet, thousands of boats work the coastal waters, which contain an abundance of fish and shellfish.

TRANSPORTATION

Korea has an advanced system of railways, well-developed highways, ferries and bus routes. Korea's first high-speed rail service began in 2004. South Korea's six largest cities—Seoul, Busan, Daegu, Gwangju, Daejeon, and Incheon—all have modern subway systems. Bicycles are a popular form of recreation and transportation in South Korea.

There are four international airports: Incheon, Jeju, Gimhae (Busan), and Yangyang in South Korea. South Korea's Korean Air and Asiana Airlines handle domestic and international flights. Incheon International Airport, South Korea's largest airport, handles about 39.2 million passengers a year. It has continually won top or close-to-top honors as the "best international airport" according to various ranking systems. Every year from 2005 to 2012, for example, it was rated the world's top airport by Airports Council International.

Air travelers wait for their flights at Incheon International Airport.

INTERNET LINKS

www.oecd.org/korea
The OECD has a wealth of statistical information about life in South Korea, including many economic topics.

english.mafra.go.kr/main.jsp
This is the site of the Ministry of Agriculture, Food and Rural Affairs.

english.visitkorea.or.kr/enu/1091_Destination.jsp
Imagine Your Korea, the site of the Korea Tourism Organization, offers destination recommendations for tourists.

ENVIRONMENT

Smog hangs over the Han River Apartment Buildings in Seoul. Through the haze, the river can be seen in the background.

5

SOUTH KOREA IS A HIGHLY industrialized nation, which is great for its economy. However, industrialization creates environmental problems, such as pollution and land use issues. Those situations, in turn, affect a country's wildlife as well as its people. Air pollution is one of South Korea's most pressing environmental concerns. Automobiles and industrial facilities are the main sources of pollutants, especially in the larger cities. Seoul has one of the highest automobile ownership rates among the nation's cities—and ownership is growing.

Heavy industries cause severe pollution in areas where they are concentrated, especially if manufacturing plants do not take care in treating and disposing of chemical waste. Among the environmental consequences of population growth has been deforestation. Korea's forests have long been harvested for fuel. Deforestation has led to floods, droughts, and the loss of wildlife.

The good news is that the South Korean government has been able to institute a sophisticated and wide-reaching environmental

"Have Korean tigers really disappeared? No. Korean tigers still live in the wild, not only a couple of them but several hundred of them. It's just that they don't live on the Korean peninsula…"
—Lee Hang, professor of Veterinary Medicine, Seoul National University, and head of the Korean Tiger and Leopard Conservation Fund

protection agency. The Ministry of Environment is devoted to the country's environmental welfare across the board, from air, water, and soil pollution issues; natural conservation matters; and waste and recycling practices to climate change concerns.

BATTLING AIR POLLUTION

South Korea's environment ministry has taken serious measures

Two women wear face masks in Seoul on a particularly bad air quality day in February 2014.

to manage the quality of air in Seoul's metropolitan region. Efforts to deal with pollution in such a densely populated area have required close cooperation between the government and the people, and not only corporations but also individuals.

The Special Act on Seoul Metropolitan Air Quality Improvement was passed in 2003 to gradually reduce the level of pollution and clear up Seoul's skies. The act essentially puts the region under strict regulations to enforce the use of methods and devices that control emissions from automobiles and industrial facilities.

In the mid-2000s, after the country replaced diesel buses and trucks with vehicles powered by cleaner, compressed natural gas, South Korea's air quality started improving. In 2012, the concentration of hazardous particulate matter in Seoul's air had been reduced from that of a decade earlier. Nevertheless, the air quality in the capital city is often labeled "unhealthy."

Part of the blame is beyond the city's control, as smog and dust blow in from China. But the city is now looking at less obvious sources of pollution to try to control what it can. A recent study reported that some ten thousand Korean barbeque joints in the city are responsible for 5 percent of the total particulate emissions and that its 1,135 bathhouses are responsible for

YELLOW DUST AND SMOG FROM CHINA

Winds that blow in from the west, across the Yellow Sea, bring unwanted gifts from Korea's neighbor on the Asian mainland. Spring winds bring the dreaded hwangsa, *or "yellow dust."*

The dust originates as fine particulate matter that is swept into the atmosphere in the Gobi Desert region of China. As it passes over Chinese industrial regions, the dust picks up heavy metals and carcinogens such as dioxins, before blowing eastward and hitting the heavily populated coastal cities of the Korean Peninsula. At high levels of concentration, the dust can cause respiratory problems, especially for the elderly, the very young, and people with chronic respiratory illnesses. When levels get dangerously high, authorities usually advise people to stay indoors. TV and radio stations and government websites offer regularly updated air-quality data.

The dust problem has grown worse with increasing desertification in Mongolia and greater industrial growth in China's cities. In 2006, the dust and sand combined with snow over South Korea to cause a rare of case of yellow snow.

A South Korean protests air pollution from China.

In addition to the dust, which tends to be a seasonal phenomenon, regular industrial smog from China's cities also crosses the sea. This smog tends to worsen in the winter months as Chinese power plants burn massive amounts of coal for heating.

Naturally, South Korea is trying to work with China to cut down on China's unintended exportation of pollutants which also cause damage to livestock and crops. In 2007, South Korea sent thousands of trees to China to be planted in a way that might help block the dust, but the initiative didn't prove to be helpful.

Breathtaking scenery is all around in Jirisan National Park.

2.5 percent. Starting in 2015, those businesses were to be treated as air-polluting facilities, meaning they can be fined for going over the emission standards.

Seoul is also pushing people to drive vehicles that run on cleaner energy, and continues to encourage the use of public transportation, carpooling, biking, and walking.

PROTECTING THE LAND

REFORESTATION Korea's reforestation programs conserve trees that have economic potential. Trees selected for reforestation tend to have short growing seasons. They must to be able to grow in the different climates of the different regions, and to be useful to the fiber, paper, and edible oil industries. Reforested areas help to control shifting sands and winds, moderate floods and droughts, and contribute to the lumber, furniture, food, perfume, and paint industries.

PROTECTED AREAS The government has set aside certain natural areas where human activity is restricted. These areas include national parks and reserves throughout the peninsula. South Korea maintains twenty-one national parks, most of which are in the mountainous regions or along the coast. The largest is Jirisan National Park in the south central region, which is also the oldest designated park. It covers 182 square miles (472 sq km) of spectacular mountain scenery and hosts some 1.5 million visitors each year. Together, national parks and preserves cover 6.6 percent of the country's land area.

THE GOAL OF A WASTEFREE SOCIETY

While incinerators pollute the air, landfills pollute the land. The South Korean government has found that the best solution to the problem of waste is reduction.

THE LAST OF THE KOREAN TIGERS

More than a century ago, Korean tigers, the largest subspecies of tiger on Earth, were plentiful on the Korean Peninsula. For centuries, the tiger has been a symbol of Korean identity, playing much the same role in that culture as the bald eagle does in the United States. When Seoul hosted the Summer Olympic Games in 1988, its mascot was Hodori, a Korean tiger.

But there are no wild tigers in South Korea. Decades of hunting, poaching, development, and war have made them extinct throughout most of the Korean Peninsula. In 1922, the last Korean tiger was hunted on Mt. Daedeuk in Gyeongju, in South Korea. Some people say the tigers still roam the northernmost mountains of North Korea—there have been sightings in the Baekdu Mountain region on the Chinese border—but there is no official count. Even if tigers exist in North Korea, the barbed wire of the DMZ would prevent them from migrating south.

Today the remaining tigers of that species are called Siberian or Amur tigers. A small population of about four hundred lives in the wild in far eastern parts of Russia, but even that protected population is subject to poaching.

Siberian tigers are popular animals on exhibit in zoos throughout the world and the population of tigers in captivity is relatively strong. The tiger is one of the species covered by the Species Survival Plan, an American program run by the Association of Zoos and Aquariums, which works to preserve the survival of species that are endangered in the wild. South Koreans would like to reintroduce their tiger into its historic homeland, not only in zoos but in the wild, and environmentalists are working toward that goal.

After the Korean War ended in a ceasefire in 1953, the armistice established the Demilitarized Zone, a corridor 2.5 miles (4 km) wide that stretches 152 miles (245 km) across the Korean Peninsula. Untouched by human interference, the war-ravaged area naturally recovered. Wild habitats rebuilt themselves and wildlife was renewed. In the western section, fallow land turned into thick prairie and shrub land. In the eastern section, lush green forests covered the mountains.

Today, some 1,100 plant species and fifty mammal species are thought to live in the zone, including some rare animals: the Asiatic Black Bear, leopard, lynx, antelope and wild sheep. Environmentalists had hoped to find tigers there, but so far have not located any. In addition there are hundreds of bird species, including eagles and cranes, and more than eighty fish species.

Both North Korea and South Korea are working toward turning the DMZ into a transboundary biosphere reserve, with financial and technical assistance from the United Nations Educational, Scientific, and Cultural Organization (UNESCO). A number of international, non-governmental groups, such as The DMZ Forum, are actively working to transform the former war zone into a permanent "Peace Park" dedicated to environmental protection of the unique region as well as peace on the Korean Peninsula.

Plans to make South Korea a wastefree nation include providing recycling companies with financial support and educating the public on recycling through pamphlets and media campaigns. Laws on the treatment of waste apply to products that become harmful to the environment when disposed of. Examples include food and beverage containers that are made from synthetic materials such as polystyrene and polypropylene.

To encourage households to recycle, a fee is charged based on the amount of waste generated by each household. Manufacturers are encouraged to use fewer synthetic materials to reduce their products' potential to generate waste from consumption. Manufacturers are also responsible for developing waste collection systems and recycling or treatment facilities.

Under Korean law, recyclable products and packaging should be clearly marked with a sticker to indicate to consumers that the materials can be recycled. Korea's recyclables list includes glass, certain plastics, steel and aluminum cans, paper, batteries, refrigerators, computers, car tires, air conditioners, and light bulbs. There should also be a collection system in the product distribution area to facilitate the movement of materials to the recycling centers.

INTERNET LINKS

www.dmzforum.org
The DMZ Forum works for the conservation of the DMZ environment as a bridge to peace between the two Koreas.

ecolocalizer.com/2008/11/24/korean-tigers-back-from-the-brink-of-extinction-but-not-in-south-korea/
Ecolocalizer has a good article on the fate of the Korean tiger.

epi.yale.edu/indicators-in-practice/air-quality-index-seoul-south-korea
"The Air Quality Index for Seoul, South Korea" is a report by the Asian Institute for Energy, Environment and Sustainability.

eng.me.go.kr/eng/web/main.do
Site of South Korea's Ministry of the Environment has official reports and statistics on a wide range of environmental matters.

SOUTH KOREANS

A woman wears a colorful, embroidered hanbok, the traditional Korean dress.

6

NATIONAL ETHNIC AND RACIAL diversity, like that which comprises the population of the United States, is a foreign concept in Korea. The population of Korea is nearly homogeneous—nearly every inhabitant of the peninsula is Korean. A scant 20,000 ethnic Chinese with long-term roots in South Korea make up the peninsula's largest minority group. However, about a half million recent immigrants from the People's Republic of China (PRC) have brought new foreigners to Korea's shores; though about 71 percent of those are Chinese citizens of Korean ethnicity.

Koreans have great ethnic pride, and they strive to preserve a single identity. While there has been cultural contact between China and Korea throughout history, ethnic mixing has been rare. Having a keen awareness of cultural and ethnic differences has enabled the Korean people to retain their homogeneity. The concept of multi-ethnic nations such as the United States runs contrary to the Korean view of statehood. The ethnic Chinese living in South Korea are not citizens but residents holding Taiwanese or PRC passports.

"I grew up in war and saw the United Nations help my country to recover and rebuild. That experience was a big part of what led me to pursue a career in public service. As Secretary-General, I am determined to see this organization deliver tangible, meaningful results that advance peace, development, and human rights."
—Ban Ki-Moon, Secretary General of the United Nations, 2007–2016

Only since the Korean War in the early 1950s has there been some degree of ethnic mixing on the peninsula. During the war, many American servicemen and Korean women married and started families. However, those unions were generally not accepted by Korean society. Children of such mixed marriages were shunned as *twigi*, a term once reserved for animal hybrids.

RACIAL DISCRIMINATION

There's a fine line between ethnic pride and racism. Some scholars of Korean history say the "pure blood" Korean attitude about ethnicity developed as a response to Chinese and then Japanese domination in the nineteenth and twentieth centuries. It helped Koreans re-establish a sense of national and cultural identity as a distinct population.

But while that sort of attitude may be workable in a "hermit nation," it is causing problems in today's South Korea. As a savvy member of the global community, South Korea plays host to people of all backgrounds in business dealings,

A biracial family enjoys a day at a local park in Seoul.

education, and tourism. Koreans' rampant racial discrimination against non-Koreans is a situation that is just starting to come under scrutiny.

In 2007, The U.N. Committee on the Elimination of Racial Discrimination reported it was "concerned that the emphasis placed on the ethnic homogeneity of Korea might represent an obstacle to the promotion of understanding, tolerance and friendship among the different ethnic and national groups living on its territory." Furthermore, it urged the South Korean government to "adopt further measures, including legislation, to prohibit and eliminate all forms of discrimination against foreigners, including migrant workers and children born from inter-ethnic unions."

Although a new, digitally-connected generation is able to experience the outside world in new ways that might eventually shift attitudes in Korea, there hasn't been much substantive change yet. There is are no South Korean laws against racial discrimination. A 2009 poll revealed that 47 percent of

Korean children were uncertain or negative on the subject of whether they could make friends with a biracial child. And in 2013, the *Washington Post* rated South Korea as one of the world's least racially tolerant countries.

OLD SOCIAL SYSTEM

During the Joseon dynasty, a hierarchical social system divided the people into different social classes and defined relations between them. The classes were determined by scholastic achievements and by occupation rather than by wealth. The social system also established an obligation to authority and deemphasized individual rights.

Korean men perform rituals to honor their ancestors.

Legal class distinctions were abolished in the 1890s, but many descendants of the social elite still benefit from their status. Class distinctions can influence marriage arrangements, political affiliations, and employment opportunities.

YANGBAN The highest class, the *yangban* (YAHNG-bahn), were the power-elite. They included the scholar-officials and military officials, and their families. Only the yangban could take the civil service examinations that measured knowledge of Confucian ideas. Passing the examinations allowed them to hold government positions. If unemployed or poor, they were prohibited from doing more menial work, but they maintained the Confucian rituals and attitudes that made them figures of authority in their village.

JUNGIN Between the yangban and the common class were the *jungin* (JAHNG-in). As physicians, interpreters, handicraft makers, artists, and military officers, the jungin served as an important link between the common people and the yangban.

BAN KI-MOON

One of the most well-known South Korean people on the international scene is Ban Ki-moon, the Secretary General of the United Nations. Ban took office on January 1, 2007, succeeding Kofi Annan, and was unanimously re-elected by the General Assembly in 2011. He is to serve through the end of 2016.

Ban was born in a small farming village in the Japanese-held Republic of Korea in 1944, before its division into two countries and before the Korean War. He attended Seoul National University, where he earned a degree in international relations from in 1970. In 1985, he earned a master's degree in public administration from the Kennedy School of Government at Harvard University.

He served as a foreign minister of South Korea under President Roh Moo-hyun, a position that greatly prepared him for his position at the U.N. The Secretary-General of the United Nations has the ability to influence debate on nearly any global issue. As such, Ban has been particularly forceful in working to empower women worldwide. He has also been a leading voice for action on climate change.

Speaking to World Climate Conference in Geneva in 2009, he said of global warming, "Our foot is stuck on the accelerator and we are heading towards an abyss."

SANGMIN The sangmin (SAHNG-min), or common people, made up about 75 percent of the population. Consisting of fishermen, merchants, farmers, and minor administrators, this large class carried the burden of all taxation.

CHONMIN The lowest class was the *chonmin* (CHOHN-min), or "despised people." They included slaves, servants, convicts, jailkeepers, shamans, actors, and entertainers.

CONTEMPORARY CLASSES

A new class structure has emerged in Korea, and it is determined by wealth. Since the end of the Korean War, city dwellers in the south have grown richer because of industrialization and economic growth. These economically comfortable Koreans make up the new middle class that includes managers, healthcare professionals, and even factory workers.

The population of urban poor is decreasing. Most are recent arrivals from rural areas. Koreans of the lower class generally live in rural areas, eking out a living by farming. Education is the key to social mobility.

INTERNET LINKS

aparc.stanford.edu/news/koreas_ethnic_nationalism_is_a_source_of_both_pride_and_prejudice_according_to_giwook_shin_20060802
"Ethnic pride source of prejudice, discrimination" originally published in *The Korean Herald*, is an interesting op-ed piece about Korean attitudes about homogenous ethnicity.

content.time.com/time/photoessays/10questions/0,30255,1869053,00.html
This is a short *Time* magazine photo essay about Ban Ki-Moon.

nytimes.com/2009/11/02/world/asia/02race.html
"South Koreans Struggle With Race" is a *New York Times* article about racial attitudes of Koreans.

www.washingtonpost.com/blogs/worldviews/wp/2013/05/15/a-fascinating-map-of-the-worlds-most-and-least-racially-tolerant-countries
"A fascinating map of the world's most and least racially tolerant countries" explores racial intolerance around the world, and includes a section on South Korea.

LIFESTYLE

A statue of Confucius honors the Chinese philosopher whose words of wisdom guide so much of Korean life.

7

THE REPUBLIC OF KOREA IS A wealthy, modern country and most of its people live fully contemporary lifestyles, enhanced by all that today's technology has to offer. But at its heart, the Korean lifestyle is profoundly traditional, influenced by guiding forces that are centuries old. While economically modern, Koreans cling to many of the customs their ancestors followed. Every aspect of South Korean society, from housing to education, from gender roles to friendships, has a Confucian slant, a slight Chinese influence, and a very identifiable Korean flavor.

CONFUCIANISM

Confucianism is not a religion. Based on the ideas of the ancient Chinese philosopher Confucius (551—479 BCE), Confucianism is a social and ethical code of behavior.

Unlike a religion, Confucianism does not involve the worship of a higher being. But like some religions, it attempts to guide human relationships and improve social and ethical conduct. As such, it is an

"Confucianism is arguably the most comprehensive and integrated humanism in world history. It is also one of the most important and significant rational ways of learning to be human .... It offers Korea the core values that will make her a standard of moral excellence in the ... world."
—Tu Weiming, ethicist and director of the Institute for Advanced Humanistic Studies at Peking University.

all-encompassing philosophy on lifestyle. The fundamental thrust of Confucianism is to maintain peace and order. It has rules for familial relationships that emphasize harmony. It stresses the importance of education and respect for authority.

The five relationships considered most important in Confucianism are father/son, ruler/subject, husband/wife, elder/younger, and friendship. Koreans are very conscious of proper behavior and the loyalty of friends.

Respect for elders is an important aspect of Korean family life.

FAMILIES AND CLANS

The Korean family structure is part of a larger kinship structure that is defined by specific obligations. The kinship system has four levels.

HOUSEHOLD The ideal Confucian family has four generations under one roof. Multigenerational households are quite common in rural areas in Korea, but urban families may not follow this pattern. Young married couples start their life together in an apartment away from their parents.

The Confucian household is made up of husband and wife, their children, and the husband's parents if he is the eldest son. This arrangement is called *jip* (jip), meaning "big house." The households of younger sons are called *chagunjip* (CHAH-gehn-jip), or "little house."

In a Korean home, the head of the family—usually the oldest male—holds the position of authority, and every family member is expected to do as he says. There is an understanding that the authority figure will always be fair in dealing with members of the household. According to Confucian ideals, the authority figure also represents, supports, and protects the family. Should he be unable to do this properly, he will lose face as the family head.

Respect for authority, a valued virtue in Confucianism, is what maintains order in traditional Korean families. In the ideal Confucian household, the

Filial piety is a child's sense of complete devotion to his or her parents. Koreans feel a strong sense of gratitude and obligation toward their parents, most intensely a man toward his father. In Confucianism, filial piety is considered even more important than a subject's observance of respect for his ruler.

Dedication to one's elders is considered an essential factor in the formation of one's personality. It is part of the idea that the family, or group, is a more important unit in the framework of society than the individual. The application of filial piety is extended in Korean society beyond parent-child relationships. It is a code of behavior relevant to interactions with all elders.

wife obeys her husband, the children obey their parents, younger siblings obey their older siblings, and so on according to the family hierarchy.

MOURNING GROUP The second level of the Korean kinship system, the *tangnae* (THANG-nay), is made up of people who have the same ancestry going back four generations on their father's side. The tangnae gathers at graveyards to perform rites that offer respect to ancestors.

LINEAGE The third level, *p'a* (pah), is the lineage that traces all the descendants of one man. Thousands of households may belong to one p'a. A p'a is not only responsible for performing ancestral rites; its members also provide aid for needier members of the group and oversee the behavior of younger members. A p'a often owns land and buildings, such as gravesites and schools, which its members can use.

CLAN The fourth level is the *tongjok* (THONG-jok). Tongjok members have the same surname, or family name. This group is so large that it generally does not have great feelings of solidarity. The most practical function of the tongjok is to determine the acceptability of marriage partners. There are strict

Childhood friendships often last a lifetime.

rules against marrying someone who shares a common ancestor on the father's side, no matter how far back. There are only about two hundred family names, and therefore as many tongjok.

FRIENDSHIP

Loyalty between friends is also very important in Korea. Friendship is one of the few equality-based relationships in Korean society. When two people become friends, they expect to stay friends for the rest of their lives.

For Koreans, most friendships date back to their schooldays—the time in most Koreans' lives when their peers are truly their equals. Within a group of boys or girls, there are no status markers to differentiate students. Each is involved in the same experience. Friends are expected to be there in times of need to support and to help solve problems. To deny a friend's request is unthinkable.

As one's friendships mature, they extend from one's personal life to include one's professional life as well. Friends are expected to provide contacts and opportunities to one another throughout their careers.

ROLE OF WOMEN

Korean society is male-dominated. Korean women traditionally hold subservient positions. Few pursue careers. The woman is considered an "inside" manager, who tends to home matters. She is the homemaker, raising the children, monitoring the household finances, and doing the daily chores. If her husband's parents live with them, she takes care of them as well as she does her husband and children.

Koreans traditionally prefer sons to daughters. In traditional Korean culture, a son carries the family line and takes over the family business, while a daughter marries into another family and bears children for that family. Even today, Korean families deciding to send their children to international schools or abroad for a Western-style education almost always send their sons rather than their daughters.

Much traditional Korean culture still forms a big part of present-day Korean society, although economic demands have changed things to some extent. The contribution of women has been essential to the tremendous economic success of South Korea. Some 59 percent of women work outside the home, yet working women in South Korea do not enjoy the same rights as their male counterparts. On average, they make 39 percent less money than men do for comparable work. Many hold low-level jobs in export-oriented industries and work long hours for low wages. However, as more women acquire a college education, more go into professional fields such as education, medicine, law, and business. But lack of education is not the main reason for employment disparity. In 2011, women made up a mere 1 percent of the nation's corporate boards.

A Korean mother holds her baby boy.

The curious counterpoint to all this, of course, is the fact that in 2013, South Korea elected a woman president. President Park Geun-Hye has established a goal of creating 1.65 million new jobs for women by February 2018. Minister of Gender Equality and Family Cho Yoon Sun encourages South Korean corporations to hire and promote more women.

MALE-FEMALE RELATIONSHIPS

In early Korean society, men and women were segregated and had little opportunity to interact with the opposite sex and develop social skills involving the opposite sex. Although Korean men and women are now freer to mingle, old practices such as matchmaking are still common. Dowries continue to play an important role in Korean marriages and involve large sums of money and family business mergers.

DRESS

Most Koreans in the cities wear Western-style clothing. Older Koreans, especially in rural areas, may wear traditional clothing. Many scoff at the modern fashions of city dwellers and take pride in wearing old-fashioned clothes. During festivals, however, most Koreans wear traditional clothing when they take part in ritual celebrations.

The traditional Korean dress is called the hanbok *(HUN-bok). It is loose-fitting for cool comfort and beautifully detailed with colors. The hanbok for men consists of bloomer-like pants called* baji *(BAH-ji), a short sleeveless jacket or vest, and a coat called a* durumagi *(doo-roo-mah-gi). The hanbok for women consists of a short jacket or blouse called a* jeogori *(JUH-go-ri) and a long skirt called a* chima *(CHI-mah). The jeogori has a long sash tied in a bow on the side.*

The modern design of the hanbok is quite similar to styles that were worn during the Joseon dynasty. There are different types of hanbok for different occasions, such as the Lunar New Year, first and sixty-first birthday celebrations, and weddings.

There are some rural areas in Korea where grandmothers, or halmoni *(HALH-muh-ni), and grandfathers, or* haraboji *(HAH-rah-buh-ji), wear traditional clothes every day and look like their ancestors in old photographs. An old man will typically have dangling amber buttons on his jacket, rubber shoes with pointed, upturned toes, and a tall hat, or* satkat *(SUD-cut), woven out of black horsehair. Old men in rural areas often have long braided hair that is knotted on top of their heads.*

Marriages were not viewed as equal partnerships until recently. The relationship between husband and wife was traditionally not a close friendship. Instead, marriages were based on the wife's respect for and obedience to her husband, who was considered the superior in the relationship. As the modern Korean woman takes her place in society, however, the traditional relationships are slowly giving way to greater equality and friendship.

KIBUN AND NUNCHI

Visitors to Korea are often surprised to learn of the importance of *kibun* (KEY-boon), or harmony, in interpersonal relationships. Some have remarked on the apparent disregard Koreans have for strangers on the street. Koreans do not have the same concept of personal space as Westerners do, and the natural shoving and bumping come across as rudeness to foreigners accustomed to more space.

Five young women enjoy some ice cream together.

Kibun can be harmed by a number of etiquette blunders, such as reprimanding a worker in the presence of others, not showing due respect to a superior, using one's left hand to pass something to a superior, or saying something negative about a person's hometown. To Koreans, preserving proper kibun is essential to accomplishment. If a person is hurt or loses pride in the course of reaching a goal, the project is considered a failure.

Maintaining kibun is a complex process. In seeking to preserve a harmonious and comfortable emotional climate, individuals have to consider the state of mind of people around them while keeping a satisfactory state of mind themselves.

Sensing the emotional pulse of others calls for another Korean way of thinking, called *nunchi* (NOON-chi). Nunchi is an intuition, or hunch, which helps one read another's state of mind. People who can easily judge the body language, tone of voice, and general demeanor of other people are better able to preserve kibun and social harmony.

Koreans have no code of behavior toward foreigners. The Confucian system does not demand respect or loyalty to people with whom one has no relationship. Only when a Korean forms a bond with a person does the latter stop being treated as a stranger, and the rules of respect and kibun come into play.

High school students take the College Scholastic Ability Test in 2012 in Seoul.

EDUCATION

As part of the Confucian heritage, education is highly valued by Koreans. Education was traditionally reserved for people of the highest class, the yangban. Today education is available to all Koreans. As a result of universal education, South Korea boasts a 98 percent literacy rate, and its students consistently rank among the best on international education tests.

There are five phases of education: one to two years in kindergarten, six in elementary school, three in middle school, three in high school, and four to six in college or university. After finishing middle, or high, school, students have several avenues to further their education. Besides the major universities, there are trade or industrial schools and evening classes in the south.

Getting a good education is considered the key to a good career and a secure future. A South Korean teenager typically studies long hours in preparation for the annual university entrance examination that will determine his or her future. Students prepare years ahead for the eight-hour examination that tests their knowledge in mathematics, history, English, chemistry, literature, and physics. The examination is the sole factor in determining whether a student will be admitted to most universities. When students fail, they have to wait a full year before applying to another university and taking the examination again. If they fail the second time, there is no third chance.

There is intense competition for university places. Parents put a lot of effort into helping their children pass the examination. They hire tutors and change their lifestyle to offer moral and financial support in the months before the examination. In the past, sisters took factory jobs to bring in extra money so that their brothers could hire tutors. Mothers wake up early in the morning to help their children begin studying. They also provide nourishing meals into the night.

Critics argue that the extreme pressure to excel academically is hurting South Korea's young. Some high-school students develop physical ailments due to anxiety and some even commit suicide because of poor scholastic results. In a 2010 survey, 53 percent of young South Koreans who confessed to feeling suicidal said their inadequate academic performance was the main reason for such thoughts.

HOUSING

The traditional Korean home is an L-shaped, U-shaped, or rectangular single-story structure. Generally, the walls are built of clay and wood and the roof of thatch or tiles. But these typical houses can only be seen in rural parts of Korea today.

In cities, high-rise apartments abound to ease the housing shortage that has resulted from rapid urban growth since the Korean War. Newer buildings are made of concrete, and houses are built to keep out cold air. Rooms are small, and doors and windows are few. Most houses have *ondol* (ON-doll), a heating system that dates back to the Stone Age. Ondol is a system of air pipes that are connected to the stove in the kitchen and pass under the floor. As the warm air from the stove passes through the pipes, it warms the floor, making it comfortable to walk or sit on.

Perhaps it is because of this heating method that most of the activities of a Korean family take place on the floor. Family members sleep and sit on mats on the floor. Even when dining, Koreans sit on the floor at low tables. Until recently there were few, if any, chairs or beds in a Korean home. Another practical custom that arose from having so much activity take place on the floor is that of always removing one's shoes before entering a home.

In this view of Seoul, autumn foliage contrasts with the rugged mountains in the background and the cityscape in the foreground.

LIFE EVENTS

BIRTH   The preference for male offspring is long-established in the patriarchal Confucian system. Korean wives have long faced a lot of pressure to bear a son to continue the family bloodline. The pressure has somewhat lessened, although the birth of a boy is still considered a greater blessing.

Because it was so important to bear a son, wives offered prayers and followed rituals in the hope of having a baby boy. Offerings were made for a hundred days to Taoist shrines, to the Buddha, and to various natural entities such as rocks and trees.

The main spirit concerned with childbirth is the *Samsin Halmeoni* (SUM-sin Hul-MO-neh), or "grandmother spirit," who provides for the child even after it is born, guiding its growth and health. Her shrine is usually found inside the house and is represented by a piece of folded paper or clean straw hung in a corner.

For three weeks after birth, a straw rope of chili peppers or pine needles known as a *kumjul* (KEHM-jool) is hung across the doorway of the house to frighten evil spirits and warn people not to enter. Seaweed soup and rice are offered to the Samsin Halmeoni every morning and evening for a week. These foods are also eaten by the mother to speed up her recovery.

The newborn's family takes special care not to show their joy over the birth, because they believe the spirits may become jealous and cause the baby harm. To mislead the spirits, Korean babies are sometimes given unbecoming names.

BIRTHDAYS Koreans celebrate their first and sixtieth birthdays, called *dol* (DOUL) and *hwangap* (HWUN-gup) respectively, in a grand way. A big party also takes place on a baby's hundredth day of life, which in the past many failed to reach.

The hundredth-day celebration, called *baegil* (PAY-gil), is quite a jubilee. It marks the baby's survival of a critical period that was once characterized by high mortality rates. Offerings of food are made to the Samsin Halmeoni, before family and friends celebrate with wine, rice cakes, and other delicacies. Finally, the guests present their gifts to the baby.

The dol, or first birthday, is celebrated in much the same way, but it is of even greater significance. Not only has the baby survived, but if it is a boy, he is ready to choose his future career.

The highlight of the event comes when the baby boy, dressed in the finest hanbok, is seated at a small table where his gifts and other items are placed. It is believed that the object that the child picks up from the table represents what he will become when he grows up. If it is a piece of string or yarn, he is supposed to live a long life. If it is money or rice, a business career awaits. If it is cake or other food, a career in government service is in the offing. If it is a musical instrument, he will become an artist. Guests leave the birthday party with packages of rice cakes given by the child's parents, who believe that sharing these rice cakes will bring the child good health and happiness.

A lucky little man celebrates his first birthday.

The celebration of the sixtieth birthday, or hwangap, arose in the past when few people lived to that age. Also, the lunar calendar used by Koreans is based on sixty-year cycles. Each year in the cycle has a different name, so when people reach their sixtieth year, the cycle returns to the year of their birth.

The family usually throws a lavish party, and loved ones gather to honor the celebrant. Rituals involve guests bowing to the celebrant and drinking wine, while traditional Korean music plays right through the party. Rice cakes and fresh fruit are served as part of the feast, and a photograph of the party group is taken to commemorate the event.

A couple dresses in modern Western attire for their wedding.

MARRIAGE Few Koreans choose not to marry, since marriage is associated with maturity in Korea. In fact, an unmarried person is called a big baby in Korean slang. There are two kinds of marriages: love marriages, or *yonae* (yo-NAY); and arranged marriages, or *chung-mae* (choong-MAY).

Chungmae are not as common in present-day Korea as they once were. The first step in an arranged marriage is for the two families to meet. The woman's parents probe the man's parents about his personality, his potential for success, and how he is likely to treat his wife. The man's parents set out to learn about the woman's character, health, and ability to fit into their family.

If the parents' meeting goes well, the young man and woman are left alone to get to know each other. They will not be forced to marry if they do not get along. But if they are compatible, they go out on a few dates and discuss their expectations of married life. When they are ready, they announce the marriage to their parents.

Regardless of whether a young Korean couple is entering into a love or arranged marriage, one or both of the mothers will probably visit a fortune-teller who will read the couple's astrological charts to check for compatibility and to determine an auspicious date for the wedding.

An engagement of two to three months is usual. In that time, both families must prepare gifts for one another.

OLD AGE Asians generally pride themselves on their care for the aged, and Koreans are no exception. With fewer extended families living in the same home, the way the elderly are cared for has changed. Nonetheless, the elderly in Korea are still treated with great respect, and children travel great distances each year to celebrate their parents' birthdays. Strangers will give up their seats for older people on buses and greet older people on the street with the appropriate honorific titles or language showing respect.

THE PROBLEM OF PATRILINEAGE

Prior to 2005, South Korea banned marriage between people of the same clan. That is, two people with the same last name and ancestral home, called dongseong dongbon, *were not allowed to marry.*

In Korea, family identities are tracked according to patrilineage, or bloodlines on the father's side, back to an originating ancestor. People whose surname and ancestral origin are the same are in the same clan. The problem is that there are relatively few family names in South Korea—fewer than three hundred in a population of about 49 million— and some clans date back two thousand years. Members of such clans number in the millions. For example, people with the surname Kim (the most popular surname in South Korea), can be divided between 282 different blood ancestors, each of whom is identified with a different ancestral home. The two most populous branches of the Kim clans are Gimhae, with four million members, and Gyeongju with 1.5 million members.

The chances of meeting and falling in love with someone from one's own clan are therefore fairly high. In the past, this spelled heartbreak for some young couples, and many broke up rather than go against tradition. Some lived together without marriage, which caused certain difficulties, and others went abroad to get married.

Both China and North Korea abolished their similar bans against intra-clan marriage before South Korea finally did in 2005. Now, only closely related couples, such as cousins and second cousins, are not allowed to marry.

Old age is a time for leisure. Many older Koreans spend their free time traveling in tour groups around the country to visit famous attractions that they have heard about but never had a chance to see.

DEATH Korean customs and rituals surrounding death are also dictated by Confucian beliefs. Because of the emphasis on respect for parents and ancestors, careful attention is given to death rituals and funerals.

Dying at home is very important to Koreans. Doctors try to provide ample notice to a family when a relative is critically ill, so they can take the patient home before death. It is bad luck to bring a dead body home.

When someone dies, the body is covered with a white quilt, and formal wailing, or *kok* (kohk), announces the death. The body is arranged so that

While most weddings in South Korea are Western-style ceremonies, some couples still marry traditionally. The bride's dowry depends on the prestige of the groom's family. The bride's family provides Western clothing for the groom's male relatives and Western clothing and traditional Korean dress for his female relatives. In addition, the bride often gives expensive jewelry to her future mother-in-law.

The groom sends the bride a ham *(HAHM), a box of gifts—jewelry and fabric for a hanbok. A friend of the groom brings the box to the bride's home at a prearranged time and shouts that he has a ham for sale. The family must coax the box from him with wine and food.*

The traditional wedding ceremony is held in the bride's home. It begins with an exchange of bows and drinks. The bride and groom face each other across a table with objects symbolizing their future together. The wedding ceremony is followed by another called the pyebaek *(PAY-back), which is the bride's first greeting to her husband's family. It is at this time that the bride presents the groom's family with their gifts.*

Afterward, the couple dresses in traditional Korean wedding clothes for official photographs and participates in bowing ceremonies to honor the marriage and the family.

it faces south, in a ritual called *chohon* (CHOH-hon). The next step is *yom* (yohm), the preparation of the corpse, which entails bathing the body in perfumed water and dressing it in ritual burial clothes.

Notice of the death is sent out, and those who receive the notice visit the home of the deceased. This visit to pay respects to the deceased and offer condolences to the surviving family members is called *munsang* (MOON-sahng). Not conveying condolences is an offense to the grieving family and can create feuds and end friendships.

The *chulssang* (CHOOL-sahng) is the carrying of the coffin to the graveyard. This is accompanied by great fanfare, with some people carrying the coffin on their shoulders, some carrying flags and incense, and others ringing bells and singing mournfully.

At the burial ground, the family performs an ancestral ritual. Once the body is positioned to face south, the oldest son throws the first handful of dirt on the coffin.

INTERNET LINKS

www.religionfacts.com/a-z-religion-index/confucianism.htm
Religion Facts offers a clear overview of Confucianism.

www.patheos.com/Library/Confucianism.html
Patheos has an in-depth section on Confuscianism.

english.mogef.go.kr/index.jsp
This is the official English language site of the Republic of Korea's Ministry of Gender Equality and Family.

lifeinkorea.com/culture/marriage/marriage.cfm
Life in Korea has a nice overview of traditional marriage in Korea, with photos.

weareteachers.com/hot-topics/special-reports/teaching-around-the-world/south-koreas-school-success
We Are Teachers, "South Korea's School Success," offers a quick comparison of South Korean and U.S. test results.

english.visitkorea.or.kr/enu/AK/AK_EN_1_4_9.jsp
The Korea Tourism Organization's "About Korea" section has a simple overview of Korean customs.

RELIGION

A happy Buddha is depicted in this golden statue at Haedong Yonggungsa Temple in Busan.

8

THE KOREAN APPROACH TO religion is varied and embraces both the very old and the very new. This is due to their long history as a people dating back thousands of years as well as the great changes to their way of life that colonial rule by Japan brought in the early twentieth century. Ancient Shamanism is embraced along with Christianity, Buddhism, and Taoism. But many South Koreans follow no religion at all.

The South Korean Constitution guarantees its citizens freedom of worship. The majority of Koreans report that they are Christian, followed by those who say they are Buddhist. But in reality, most Koreans mix those beliefs and rituals with those of shamanism, an ancient form of spirit worship that is entrenched in the Korean way of life. For example, some Buddhist temples in Korea are carved with the figures of shamanist deities, and in the Korean version of the Christian Bible, the word "God" is translated as *hanamin*, as the "great spirit" in shamanism is known.

HISTORY

With the fall of the Joseon Dynasty at the end of the nineteenth century, and the colonization of the Korean Peninsula by Japan, huge cultural changes took place. Japan felt that Korean culture was "backwards"

"The purpose of a fishtrap is to catch fish, and when the fish are caught, the trap is forgotten. The purpose of a rabbit snare is to catch rabbits. When the rabbits are caught, the snare is forgotten. The purpose of words is to convey ideas. When the ideas are grasped, the words are forgotten. Where can I find a man who has forgotten words? He is the one I would like to talk to."
—Chuang-Tzu, (399–295 BCE), Buddhist sage

and needed to be modernized. Christianity took root at this time with the arrival of Protestant missionaries. Christianity became part of a nationalist movement for Korean identity as it was in opposition to Japan's effort to promote the Japanese religion of Shintoism and the Japanese language.

Once the Japanese were removed from colonial rule after surrendering to the Allies after World War II, the stage was set for Korea to become a multi-religious society. With the shift in power came a new era that made it possible for old religions such as Buddhism, Shamanism, and Confucianism to co-exist with new religions such as Christianity, Daejong-gyo, and Cheondo-gyo.

A wooden totem like this one traditionally marked villages boundaries and acted as a guardian.

SHAMANISM

Shamanism is a system of beliefs and practices that honor the spirits of nature. Korea's earliest form of religion does not aim for moral perfection. Shamanists believe that spirits inhabit everything, living and nonliving, and that spirits can pass between humans, plants, rocks, animals, and other objects.

Shamans, or *mudang* (MOO-dung), are usually women who act as intermediaries between people and spirits. They are believed to be able to influence spirits. Mudang are especially interested in the spirits of the dead and help resolve conflicts between the living and the dead. They perform ancient ceremonies to predict a brighter future for a person, cure illnesses by exorcising evil spirits, and help guide spirits to heaven.

BUDDHISM

Buddhism is the second most prominent religion in South Korea with 24 percent of the population identifying as Buddhist, after Christianity

A PROBLEM-SOLVING INTERVENTION: THE KUT

In any culture, people have problems, and from one culture to another, there are many ways to try to solve them. In South Korea, women called mudang *are shamans who take a spiritual approach to solving the problems of life. They hold* kut *(KOOD), or services to help cure illness, exorcising evil spirits, or even to help guide the soul of a deceased person. The goal is to strengthen relationships among family members and the spirit world. If the problem worsens instead, the diagnosis is that the gods want to play or the family's ancestors are angry at certain family members.*

The kut is a noisy ceremony, filled with shouting and the clanging of gongs. There is also singing, dancing, and chanting. The ceremony is a request to the gods or the ancestors to enjoy the festive atmosphere. This, it is believed, dispels all ill-will.

At some point in the service, the mudang lapses into a trance and acts as the receptacle of the spirits. She speaks to the gods or the ancestors, who speak back through her. As the service progresses, all the women of the household, and even friends and neighbors, participate by shouting to the supernatural visitors. Angry ancestors who cause illness can be exorcised by tossing grain, while angry gods can only be appeased with offerings and treats.

The kut may be held at the house of the person hiring the shaman, at the shaman's own home, or even outdoors, because the service must adapt to the type of problem it is addressing. The ceremony often goes on all night, and as day breaks, the shaman and her aides beat drums and perform a final exorcism for good luck.

A mudang in a traditional costume performs a dance to chase away evil spirits during a blessing ceremony on the Han River in Seoul.

The bronze Great Unification Buddha sits 62 feet high (18.9 meters) in quiet meditation at Sinheungsa Temple.

with 32 percent of the population. Across the Korean Peninsula, there are thousands of Buddhist temples.

Buddhism began in Korea during the Three Kingdoms period. The religion is based on the teachings of the Buddha, Siddhartha Gautama, who was the prince of a small Indian kingdom in the sixth century. The basic idea of Buddha's teachings is that enlightenment and personal freedom comes from giving up worldly desires and living in moderation. By living according to the Buddha's teachings, a Buddhist believes that he or she can reach the state of nirvana, ultimate peace, wherein a person experiences no pain or worry.

There are two main schools of Buddhism: Theravada and Mahayana. Korean Buddhism belongs to the Mahayana school, which is tolerant of local spiritual practices and puts no restriction on one's ability to reach salvation. Because Buddhism has been a part of the religious fabric of Korea for so many years, it has been mixed with some aspects of other religions, such as shamanism.

In fact, nearly every Buddhist temple in Korea has a chapel next to it that contains a shrine dedicated to the spirit of the local mountain. The shrine receives the same respect that is bestowed on Buddhist shrines. This is done to avoid angering the local mountain spirit, upon whose land the Buddhist temple sits.

CHRISTIANITY

Christianity was brought to Korea in the sixteenth century by Confucian intellectuals who learned about it in the Chinese capital, Peking (present-day Beijing). However, the new teaching caused problems. New converts to Christianity refused to participate in ancestral rites, so the Korean government tried to prevent Christian missionaries from entering the country.

The first half of the nineteenth century was a difficult time for Korean Christians. Thousands were persecuted, and many were beheaded. Nonetheless, by 1865, there were more than 20,000 Catholics in Korea. Today, with Christians making up about 31 percent of the population (Protestants 24 percent, Catholic 7.6 percent), South Korea is second only to the Philippines among Asian nations in its percentage of Christians.

A Catholic church in Inje

There are numerous denominations of Christianity, such as the Methodists and Presbyterians, in Korea. Most Protestant denominations in Korea are fundamentalist. Protestant fundamentalism emphasizes the literal interpretation of the Bible as essential to Christian life. There are also several minor Christian groups that some consider to be cult-like. A cult is generally described as a religious group devoted to a living leader or an unusual practice or teaching.

INTERNET LINKS

www.korea.net/AboutKorea/Korean-Life/Religion
This is the official website of the Korean Department of Global Communications and Content.

asiasociety.org/countries/religions-philosophies/historical-and-modern-religions-korea
The Asia Society's "Historical and Modern Religions of Korea" section offers a solid overview of religion in Korea.

www.pbs.org/hiddenkorea/religion.htm
This text accompanies the DVD, "Hidden Korea," and explores the culture of the Republic of Korea.

LANGUAGE

Hangeul, the Korean writing system, is unusual in that it was deliberately created to be easy to read and write.

9

I N KOREAN, THE WORD FOR THE Korean language is *Kugo*. The origins of the language are obscure and linguists enjoy arguing over its source. Although the Korean Peninsula connects to the Chinese land mass, the roots of its language are completely different from that of the Chinese languages. Most language experts agree that Korean originated in central Asia in the Altai Mountains. It bears a resemblance to other languages in the Altaic family, such as Turkish, Mongolian, and the Manchu-Tungus languages of Siberia. Some linguists even include the Uralic languages of Finnish and Hungarian as having the same linguistic roots.

Although Chinese belongs to a separate language family, it has had a tremendous influence on Korean; half of the Korean vocabulary is derived from Chinese. But grammatically, Korean resembles Japanese. One thing about the Korean language is clear, though. It has a logical writing system, *hangeul*, deliberately invented in the fifteenth century,

A Korean proverb says: 가는 말이 고와야오는 말이 곱다.
Pronunciation: "Ga-neun mali gowa-ya oneun gop-da."
Literal meaning: "If the outgoing words are beautiful, then the incoming words will be beautiful too."
Similar saying in English: "Treat others as you would have them treat you."

and it's possibly the single most important thing that ever happened in Korea, because it brought literacy to the masses.

Regional Korean dialects are similar except for a few words that are pronounced slightly differently. South Korea's official dialect is the one used in the region of Seoul. Koreans living in different parts of the peninsula can usually communicate using their own dialects. The people of Jeju Island are the exception.

Korea's well-established social structure and its etiquette system call for different levels of language to appropriately distinguish between individuals and social classes. There are three language levels in use: a very polite form to address superiors; a personal form for speaking to equals or close friends; and a common or humble form for addressing people of a lower social level, or when referring to oneself.

Scholars from South Korea and North Korea hold a joint conference in Seoul to discuss how to make a new Korean-language dictionary to be used in both Koreas.

HANGEUL

Sejong, the Joseon king from 1418 to 1450, was responsible for the development of hangeul. He wanted to enable all Korean people to write in their language. In his time, only the upper classes were educated and could decipher the Chinese characters representing the Joseon language.

Sejong faced great opposition to the project. Officials and scholars feared that Korean literature would be degraded—brought down to the level of dust—if it could be produced and understood by everyone. However, the king persisted, believing in literacy for all.

Hangeul was first known as *hunmin jeongeum*, or "the right sounds for the instruction of the people." Sejong appointed scholars to devise a user-friendly alphabet system that closely represented the sounds of the Korean language as it was spoken then. The system was designed to be easy to read and write.

Hangeul uses a phonetic system of twenty-four characters: fourteen consonants and ten vowels. Each character represents a specific sound. Typically, two consonants sandwich a vowel between them to form a syllable. The twenty-four characters combine in many different ways to represent thousands of sounds and words in the Korean language.

A market sign in both Korean and English in Seoul

Hangeul is easier to learn than many languages, including English. There are no capital letters, and vowels and consonants are easily differentiated. To the untrained eye, handwritten hangeul may look like squiggles, but painted with a brush in calligraphy, hangeul looks like art.

VOCABULARY

As is the case with most modern languages, the Korean language consists of indigenous words and words borrowed from foreign languages. Many English words, such as *aspirin*, *supermarket*, and *bus*, have crept into the Korean language. Scientific and technological terms make up the majority of borrowed Western words.

Most borrowed words in Korean speech and writing come from the Chinese language, because Koreans have had contact with the Chinese for thousands of years. Chinese words assimilated into Korean are often called Sino-Korean words. Sino-Korean is to the Koreans what French is to the old aristocracies of Europe, a kind of elitist language.

Chinese numbers are generally used, especially after the numeral 10 and when counting items in successive order, such as in money and months.

STRUCTURE

In the Korean language, affixes add meaning to a root word or show its grammatical function. Verbs are generally the last element in a sentence, while the other parts can be switched around freely.

Like Japanese, Korean has no articles (*a, an, the*), and singular and plural forms are usually the same. Also, the subject of a sentence is not mentioned when it seems apparent. For example, "Are you going?" and "Are they going?" would be asked in exactly the same way.

NAMES

Most Koreans have three names: the family name and two given names. The family name appears first. The first given name usually identifies one's generation and may be shared by siblings and cousins. The second given name may be a personality trait. Sons sometimes get one of their father's given names. For example, Kim Jong Il's second given name was the first given name of his father, the late North Korean president Kim Il Sung.

Koreans often consult shamans and sages before naming their babies. Choosing the right name is considered instrumental in bringing a person good fortune. Many Korean parents name their children after positive characteristics, such as "wise" or "lovely," hoping that their children will grow up to personify their names.

Despite the fact that there are nearly three hundred Korean surnames, half the population are Parks, Kims, or Lees. Some other relatively common family names in Korea are Shin, Han, Oh, Chang, and Choi.

Korean women do not change their family name when they marry. A woman may be addressed as Mrs. Min in conversation, since that is her husband's surname, but she is really known by her birth name throughout her life. She may also be called *ajumoni* (ah-JOO-moh-ni) or *puin* (POO-in), which both mean something like "madam" or "aunty." Once a woman has a child, this form of address is replaced by one that indicates her new status. For example, if her oldest child is Sang-jun, she will be called Sang-jun's mother, even when he is an adult.

It is disrespectful to address the elderly by their given names. Generally, only family members and very close friends call a person by the given name.

TITLES

Titles are very important, because Koreans cannot communicate in the correct manner if they do not know the social status of the people they interact with. Titles are also necessary where many people share the same family name. For example, if several employees in a large company share the name Lee, the use of titles such as Director and Supervisor before the family name helps to avoid confusion. Titles may also reveal information about birthplace, schools, and so on, so that the proper measure of respect is shown when speaking to a superior.

An elderly Korean couple dress in traditional hanbok at a festival in Seoul.

HONORIFICS

Honorifics are polite forms of address reserved for older members of society or people of a higher social class. The most polite way to greet an older or more senior person in Korea is *ann-yong-ha-shim-ni-ga* (AHN-yong-HAH-shim-NI-kah).

Honorifics also flatter. A Korean may address another as *Yangban*, an ancient title of nobility, just as a Westerner may address another as Boss. The title *Paksa* (PAK-sah), for teacher, may be used to address someone who has been offended, in the hope that he or she will assume the self-restraint expected of teachers and not be justly angry.

NONVERBAL COMMUNICATION

While certain behaviors, such as laughing or crying, are basic human reactions and convey the same emotive meaning all over the world, many nonverbal

forms of communication are culture-bound and convey a specific meaning that only an understanding of the culture can interpret correctly.

BOWING   Koreans bow when they meet and when they part. The person of lower status will bow first and say a greeting. Then the other person quickly bows and responds in kind. If the person being greeted is of much higher status (for example, a father receiving a greeting from his son), he may not bow, responding instead with an intimate greeting.

Bows range from a slight tilt to a right-angle bend to touching the ground. The greater the angle of the bow, the greater the respect shown. Someone who lowers his or her head all the way to the ground, palms touching the floor, shows the greatest degree of respect. This gesture is used in temples or homes, not in the office or on the street.

From the way two Koreans greet each other, an observer can easily distinguish the teacher, the doctor, and the grandfather from the student, the patient, and the grandson.

HAND GESTURES Korean hand gestures can be quite different from those used in the United States. For example, the wave that a North American understands as goodbye is the Korean signal to approach the waver. To wave goodbye, Koreans wave their raised forearm side to side, palm facing out. The American gesture for come, with the palm facing upward is used by Koreans only to call a dog. The way to call a person closer is to extend the arm with the palm downward, making a scratching motion.

Koreans use the right hand to pass an object to a superior. To show more respect, they use the left palm to support the right elbow. The greatest respect is shown by handing an object to a superior with both hands. Using the right hand is so associated with respect that children showing a tendency toward left-handedness are encouraged to rely more on their right hand.

FACIAL EXPRESSION While Westerners try to maintain eye contact throughout a conversation, Koreans make eye contact only some of the time. When they are not looking into the eyes of the person they are conversing with, they will look to either side of the person's face, but not higher or lower.

People of higher status maintain eye contact longer than people of lower status do. Only in an argument or when transacting business do Koreans maintain constant eye contact. When being scolded, Koreans look down slightly. However, the eye-contact rule does not apply to strangers, and Koreans may stare at strangers if they are curious about them, a behavior some foreigners may find disconcerting.

Koreans smile when they are happy as well as when they are embarrassed or uncomfortable. A person who has displeased a superior may smile the whole day. When laughing, Korean women often cover their mouths.

INTERNET LINKS

www.omniglot.com/writing/korean.htm
Omniglot is a great site for learning about any language.

www.bbc.co.uk/languages/other/korean
This BBC site includes twenty common phrases in audio version and some fast facts about the language and the alphabet.

business.uni.edu/buscomm/internationalbuscomm/world/asia/southkorea/southkorea.html
Although aimed at the business traveler, this site offers a very interesting look at Korean communication styles.

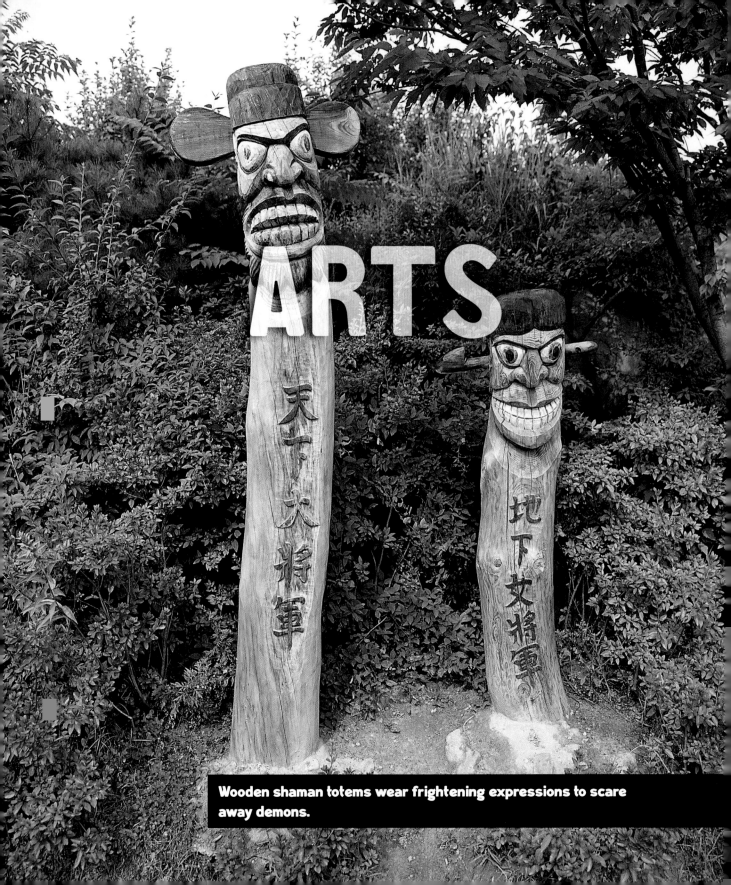

ARTS

天下大将軍

地下女将軍

Wooden shaman totems wear frightening expressions to scare away demons.

10

KOREA HAS A LONG HISTORY
and tradition of art making.
Archaeologists have found Neolithic
pottery dating back nine thousand years.
In the twenty-first century, Korea is still
producing art that commands worldwide
attention. From Stone Age pottery to
today's K-Pop music videos, the creative
arts are clearly an important part of
Korean culture.

A Korean pot found in Busan dates to the Neolithic era.

"Gangnam is a
territory in Seoul,
Korea. I describe
it as noble at the
daytime and going
crazy at the night
time. I compare
ladies to the
territory. So—noble
at the daytime,
going crazy at the
night time—and the
lyric says I am the
right guy for the
lady who is like
that."
—Korean pop star
PSY (aka Park
Jae-sang, b. 1977),
explaining the lyrics
to his hit single,
"Gangnam Style"

The pale green glaze of celadon is characteristic of certain Korean ceramics.

Korean art has been largely influenced by Japan and China. While these countries share many characteristics in the arts, each has developed distinctive features. Korean arts usually revolve around such themes as love for nature, loyalty to the king, and admiration for learning. Korea's most developed art forms include sculpture, pottery, painting, music, dance, and poetry. Simplicity and harmony with nature are recurrent characteristics that endure across all periods of Korean art.

ANCIENT ARTS AND CRAFTS

POTTERY Flat-bottomed pottery called *yunggi-mun* from the Neolithic era is intricately decorated with impressed patterns. The pottery was fired over open pit fires, and used in the daily activities of food storage and preparation. During the Iron Age, around 300 BCE, Korean pottery advanced with the development of the potter's wheel and special kilns built into hillsides that allowed for a hotter fire and sturdier ware.

Perhaps the best-known of Korea's clay arts is its celadon pottery. Celadon was first produced in Korea around 1050 CE. Koryo celadon, as it's called, uses a delicate feldspar-based glaze containing 3 percent iron. When fired at an extremely high temperature on porcelain—a fine, white clay—it produces a watery blue-green color that is now iconic. Around the twelfth century, potters began adding detailed inlay designs of cloud and crane motifs or chrysanthemums. Nearly every major art museum in the Western world has examples of Korean celadon ware.

One of the truly exceptional Korean metalcraft products is bells, or beomjong. Korean bells are sounded by striking the outer surface of the bell with a hammer, as opposed to Western bells that are sounded by an internal hammer known as a clapper. These bells ring with a deeply resonating sound that plays a role in Buddhist tohought. The best of these bells date to the Silla dynasty (668–917 CE). The Bronze Bell of Sangwon-sa Temple, from 725 CE, one of the most famous bells, is listed as Korean National Treasure No. 36.

The Bell of King Seongeok, the largest bell in Korea, was cast in 771 CE, and is Korea's National Treasure No. 29. A haunting and disturbing legend is associated with the bell: The first time the bell was cast, it made no sound, and further recasting produced the same result. A monk dreamed that the bell required a human sacrifice—and on the next casting, a baby girl from the nearby village was thrown into the molten metal. Sure enough, the resulting bell rang with an astonishing tone. It clearly sounded the mournful cry of an infant crying, "Mama!"

Beomjong is one of the four "Buddhist Instruments." The others are the dharma drum, the cloud-shaped gong, and the wooden fish. Each makes a unique sound representing the four realms of living creatures. The dharma drum is for land creatures; the wooden fish is for aquatic creatures; and the cloud-shaped gong is for creatures of the air. But the bell is for all sentient beings in the universe. Its ring, therefore, must resonate far and long, to the ends of creation.

The Bronze Bell of Sangwonsa Temple

Buddha sits atop a lotus flower in this wall painting in Gaesimsa Temple in Seosan.

METALCRAFT The development of bronze casting began around 1,000 BCE, and by 100 BCE it was a refined art. A great number of ancient bronze relics have been uncovered in Korea, including swords, spearheads, and daggers, as well as personal items such as mirrors, bells, and rattles. In time, artisans learned to work with precious metals, gold and silver, crafting crowns, earrings, necklaces, rings and other adornments. These were buried with their well-to-do owners in mounds called dolmens.

PAINTING

The early Korean painters were influenced by the Chinese. Chinese-style Korean wall paintings dating back to 400 CE have been found in tombs in Goguryeo (present-day North Korea). The bright-colored paintings depict the peoples and lifestyles of Korea some two thousand years ago. Some paintings have Chinese mythical figures, such as the sun, the moon, and dragons.

Korean landscape painting developed its own natural form during the Joseon dynasty (fourteenth to nineteenth centuries CE). Distinctive styles of composition and treatment of space emerged, as did brush-stroke techniques. A defining characteristic is the use of ink and brush on paper scrolls and screens. A reverence for flowers, mountains, rivers, and streams is expressed during this period.

Korean folk painting was overlooked for centuries because it was produced by the less educated classes. Confucian scholars spurned the colorful works of the common people, because they did not reflect the "correct" religious and intellectual values. It was customary to destroy or bury old paintings whenever new ones were created, so many old folk paintings were lost forever.

K-POP

Korean Pop Music, or K-Pop as it is commonly known, is currently Asia's hottest music industry. Encompassing all forms of contemporary music, it includes dance-pop, pop ballad, electronic, rock, hip-hop, and R&B. Fans all over the world follow the K-Pop stars' dance moves and catchy tunes. Time *magazine called K-Pop "South Korea's Greatest Export." In 2012, K-Pop broke into the Western media with the release of Psy's huge hit, "Gangnam Style," which became the most viewed video on YouTube, and the first one to hit a billion views. Other popular stars are Girls' Generation, a nine-member girl group; 2NE1 (to anyone or twenty-one), a four-member girl group; and Shinhwa, a six-member boy band that has been performing since 1998.*

Psy performs his famous hit, "Gangnam Style."

Minhwa (MIN-hoo-wa), Korea's folk paintings, give a real view of everyday life. The main theme of minhwa is the relationship between people and their environment—a theme that is expressed in Buddhism, Taoism, shamanism, and Confucianism. Minhwa is seen as a true indigenous artistic expression of the Korean people.

MUSIC

There are two kinds of traditional Korean music: *jeongak* (CHONG-gak) and *minsogak* (MIN-soh-gak). Jeongak, for the noble people, includes Confucian music, court music, and secular music of Chinese origin. Minsogak, for the common people, includes shaman music, Buddhist music, folk songs, pansori, and instrumentals called *sanjo* (SAN-joh). Folk songs vary from region to region, but common to all are the shaman and Buddhist elements.

PANSORI

Korean narrative opera, known as pansori *(PAHN-soh-ri), is an art form that captures the character and culture of Korea by teaching traditional virtues through a story. An example of a pansori is the popular story of a young woman who withstands persecution to remain faithful to a noble admirer. The story touches on the important Korean qualities of loyalty, brotherly love, friendship, and respect for parents.*

In pansori, a single performer beats out rhythms on a drum while vocalizing the roles and reciting the narrative between the songs. A complete pansori can last up to six hours.

Korea's best-known pansori performer, the master drummer Kim Myung Hwan (1913–1989), was declared a living national treasure by the government in 1978.

While always considered a vital Korean art form, pansori has recently experienced a revival among students, some of whom have embraced it in rebellion against Western art forms. Other students draw on the techniques of this traditional drama format to satirize the contemporary political scene.

Music for farming dances is probably the oldest known Korean folk music, handed down from generation to generation since the Three Kingdoms period. The original purpose of this form of music was to appease the spirits of nature, but it later took on another function—entertainment—in addition to serving as a way to influence the spirits.

Nonetheless, some Koreans still believe folk music to have a positive effect on the spirits, and farmers still perform their traditional songs and dances to ensure a good harvest, purify the village's drinking water, or protect their homes.

DANCE

Traditional Korean dances have a close connection to agricultural cycles, having probably evolved from the shaman rituals that were performed more than three thousand years ago to invoke the spirits.

Korean dances differ from most Western dances in at least one aspect: there is no choreography. Traditional Korean dances are supposed to be spontaneous and improvisational. A Korean dance does not tell a story as much as it conveys feelings. To do that, the dance involves two key concepts: *hung* (hahn) and *mot* (mot). Hung is a state of mind, an inner feeling or mood, while mot is grace and spiritual inspiration. To achieve hung and mot, the dancers have to rely more on their inner resources than on formulated dance techniques.

In traditional Korean dances, the arms and upper torso play a much greater role than the feet, which are often hidden under billowing skirts. Dance steps and poses are rare. Instead, there is a fluidity to the motion, which, combined with the airy costumes, gives the impression that the dancers are floating.

Korean dance can be broadly divided into two kinds: court and folk. Court dances are performed by both men and *kisaeng*, or female entertainers. Court dances were once performed solely for a royal audience. The elaborate costumes contrast with the simple steps.

There are two types of court dance, one of Korean origin and the other of Chinese origin. The most popular court dance is called *Hwaganmu* (HWA-kwan-moo), or "Flower Crown Dance," for which the dancers wear flowered crowns.

Folk dances are the most representative of Korean dances and can be divided into religious dances, which are led by monks, and secular dances, which are performed by ordinary people. Farming dances, in which dancers spin wildly to the beat of drums and gongs, are the oldest surviving dances

Dancers perform Korea's traditional mask dance at the Kyungbok Palace in Seoul as part of a folk art festival.

in Korea. Folk dances continue to be performed to welcome good spirits and drive away evil.

The best-known of the religious dances are the shaman dances that invoke the spirits to send the *mudang*, or shaman, into a trance. Others in the religious category are Confucian dances—stiff, ceremonial forms that were first performed in China. Confucian dances are performed at shrines in Korea during ceremonies in spring and winter.

Perhaps the most distinctive of all Korean folk dances are the mask dances. They were originally a means for people to express anger and disappointment toward the government and clergy. The themes of mask dances include corruption, greed, hypocrisy, stupidity, and fraud. The masks are the focus of the satirical dramas. Drums, cymbals, and flutes provide the musical accompaniment. The masks are burned after each performance, because it is thought that the spirits contaminate them. During the Japanese occupation, many of the dance schools died out and many dances were lost. Korean dance is enjoying a new resurgence and is taught in universities both in South Korea and abroad. Top dancers are recognized as "National Living Treasures."

CALLIGRAPHY

Calligraphy is an art form more highly regarded than painting in Korea, China, and Japan. Throughout history, calligraphy has had a strong influence on Korean culture. It is taught in schools by masters of calligraphy.

Calligraphy is the composition of characters in an aesthetically pleasing manner. Although hangeul, the Korean writing system, was invented in the mid-1400s, Chinese was used as the official script until the late 1800s.

As Confucianism and its focus on the importance of education developed during the Joseon period, calligraphy became a cherished skill. Among the nobility, the only class that knew how to write, calligraphy was considered an essential discipline for a refined gentleman.

Truly artistic calligraphy depends on the creativity and talent of the writer, who can render interesting shapes to the strokes of the written characters. Each stroke must be perfect—there is no retouching or shading—

and balanced, which requires skill that can only come with years of practice. Communication is not the main thrust of calligraphic writing. Rather, it is admired in its totality as a well-executed piece of art. This exquisite, stylized writing is considered an art form closely related to painting and is hung on walls as paintings are displayed.

Schoolmaster Hee Chin Suk teaches calligraphy to boys aged five to twenty years old in the village of Cheonghak-dong (Blue Crane). Following tradition, the students and teachers never cut their hair.

INTERNET LINKS

www.korea.net
The official website of the Republic of Korea; select "About Korea" and "Culture and the Arts."

english.visitkorea.or.kr/enu/1071_Culture.jsp
Cultural information from the official Korea Tourism Organization.

www.metmuseum.org/toah/hi/te_index.asp?i=11
The Metropolitan Museum of Art offers several in-depth pages with imagery about historic arts in Korea.

world.kbs.co.kr/english/program/program_tmusic_detail.htm?no=103946
KBS World has a page devoted to the pansori master drummer Kim Myung-hwan.

www.newyorker.com/magazine/2012/10/08/factory-girls-2?currentPage=all
"Factory Girls," from *The New Yorker* is a long article on the making of the K-pop industry.

LEISURE

Kite flying is a popular pastime in Korea. Here, hundreds of kites fill the sky at a South Korean peace festival held near the 38th Parallel in 2005.

11

T HE KOREAN WORK WEEK IS ONE OF the longest in the world, leaving little leisure time. But Koreans bring the same intense attitude they apply at work to sports, television, and nightlife. Seoul is a leisure time destination in itself—it is remarkably clean and offers activities such as shopping, meeting friends at coffee shops, or singing Korean songs at a karaoke bar.

Locals and tourists alike enjoy visiting the Dongdaemun Market, a commercial district which has more than twenty malls and 30,000 individual shops. The market is open from 10:30 am until 5:00 am, with some stores staying open twenty-four hours. Seoul also boasts the world's biggest theme park, Lotte World, where a monorail connects the outdoor Magic Island to a vast indoor theme park.

DEVOTION TO WELL-BEING

Koreans often make time to visit their local *jimjilbang*, a combination sauna, spa, and entertainment facility devoted to beauty and health. Men, women, and children enjoy the relaxing scrub downs, massages, soaking pools, and wide variety of beauty treatments. The Shinto-Buddhist bathhouse ritual, which is an important part of Japanese culture, caught on in Korea during the time of Japanese rule.

The Lunar New Year is kite-flying season, and on the last day of the new moon, people traditionally let their kites go, hoping that bad luck will float away with them.

It stands to reason that a society with such a high-pressure work culture would need intense relaxation. In addition, South Koreans value physical appearance as an indicator of a person's total well-being. People strive for physical perfection and a narrow beauty ideal that celebrates similarity rather than individuality. In fact, many brands of women's clothing have no sizes; one size is expected to fit all; or rather, all women are expected to fit the one size.

SPORTS

The popularity of sports in Korea has increased steadily. Koreans are health-conscious and highly competitive. They consider athletic activity essential to physical development and involve their children in sports—friendly or competitive—very early in life.

SOCCER South Korea has one of the most successful Asian teams and has participated in eight consecutive and nine overall FIFA World Cup tournaments, the most for any Asian team. The Korean national football team reached round 16 of the 2010 FIFA World Cup.

BASEBALL Baseball came to Korea in 1905 with Christian missionaries from the United States. Today, national baseball tournaments are major events that draw large crowds in South Korea. A baseball league was established in the 1980s, and in 1984 South Korea showed its ability to compete internationally when it won the World Little League title. The sport reached a new level of popularity when pitcher Chan Ho Park made his debut for the Los Angeles Dodgers in 1994. Park achieved a great deal of success in his Major League Baseball career, and paved the way for the American success of fellow Korean players such as Hee Seop Choi, Byung Hyun Kim, Jung Bong, Shin-Soo Choo, and Hyun-Jin Ryu.

Major-league clubs include nine professional teams among them are the Kia Tigers, the Samsung Lions, and the Doosan Bears, sponsored by large corporations such as Kia Motors and Samsung. The clubs are members of the

Jang Won-Jun of South Korea pitches during the World Baseball Classic match between Chinese Taipei and South Korea in 2013.

One of the brightest stars in Korean sports is Kim Yuna (b. 1990). She became a superstar in women's figure skating and today is one of the most highly recognized athletes and media figures in South Korea.

In February 2010, Kim competed in the Winter Olympic Games in Vancouver, British Columbia, Canada, where she won the gold medal. She became the first Korean skater to medal in any Olympic figure skating discipline. Her gold medal was South Korea's first medal at the Winter Olympics in something other than speed skating or short track. Kim's combined scores were the highest ever recorded and were entered into the Guinness Book of World Records.

Before the Olympics, she first appeared on the world senior-level skating stage when she won the bronze medal at 2006 Skate Canada. She continued to compete internationally, winning many important international skating competitions. Since 2007, she has held the world record in ladies' free skate total score.

As a result of her accomplishments, Kim is often referred to as "Queen Yuna" by media across the world. During the 2014 Winter Olympics in Sochi, Russia, she won a silver medal. At that time, Kim announced that she would end her competitive skating career.

Kim Yuna performs during her farewell ice show at Olympic Gymnastics Stadium on May 6, 2014 in Seoul.

Chang Hye Jin of South Korea releases an arrow to win the women's final at the Archery World Cup 2014.

Korean Baseball Organization, which markets the teams and organizes annual competitions.

At the 2008 Summer Olympics, the South Korean national baseball team won the gold medal in a final victory against Cuba. Currently, the South Korean men's baseball team is ranked eighth in the IBAF World Rankings. Their fans are nicknamed "Blue Bogy."

VOLLEYBALL Another twentieth-century import to Korea is volleyball. It is played by men and women professionally. Korean men's and women's volleyball teams compete in the Asian Games and other international competitions. Koreans are also recruited to coach volleyball teams in other countries.

ARCHERY Archery is one of Korea's oldest sports, one in which women can participate without fear of criticism. Today, Korean students and working adults can join clubs registered with the Korea Traditional Archery Association. Members take part in competitions that rank them according to the number of hits they make.

TAE KWON DO A self-defense martial art that originated in Korea more than two thousand years ago, tae kwon do is considered Korea's national sport. Nearly every Korean man will take up the sport at some point in his life. Tae kwon do has become popular around the world. Korean tae kwon do instructors train people in many countries. It is now an Olympic event, the only one that originated in Korea.

WRESTLING *Ssireum* (SEE-rehm), meaning the competition of man, is a Korean form of wrestling similar to Japanese sumo wrestling. Ssireum is believed to have originated as a means of self-defense more than 1,500 years ago. Over time, it became a sport. Ssireum has simple rules. Each contestant twists and turns, pushes and pulls, until one manages to force a part of the other's body to touch the ground. Ssireum is a favorite physical activity among fishermen and farmers. It is also taught in Korean middle and high schools.

OTHER SPORTS Other sports that are played and enjoyed in Korea include golf, boxing, tennis, table tennis, rifle-shooting, and skiing.

Elderly women practice tae kwon do at a gymnasium in Incheon.

INTERNET LINKS

www.korea.net/AboutKorea/Sports/Traditional-Sports
This is the official website of the Korean Ministry of culture, sports, and tourism.

www.lifeinkorea.com/activities/index.cfm
Part of the Life in Asia series of websites, it features activities and events, cultural, and shopping information.

english.visitkorea.or.kr/enu/CU/CU_EN_8_2_1_1.jsp
The Korean Tourism Organization has a page about tae kwon do.

www.nytimes.com/2014/02/09/travel/a-look-at-koreas-culture-from-the-bathhouse.html
"A Look at Korea's Culture From the Bathhouse" is an intriguing *New York Times* article about South Korea's spa and beauty culture.

FESTIVALS

A boy spins a burning can to celebrate the first full moon of the Lunar New Year in Seoul.

12

KOREAN TRADITIONAL FESTIVALS honor ancient rituals that have been celebrated for millennia. The changing phases of the moon, the movement of the seasons, and an appreciation of the numbers in a calendar date are the touchstones of the most important celebrations. The traditional Korean calendar is a lunisolar calendar, meaning it is structured around both the moon phases and the time of the solar year.

The western Gregorian calendar was adopted in Korea in 1896 for regular life activities, but observances and festivals still fall on the lunar schedule. With increasing Westernization, Koreans have developed mixed styles of celebration, incorporating certain aspects of modern urban lifestyles, such as fashion and food, into the celebration of some traditional festivals.

NEW YEAR'S DAY

New Year's Day occurs twice a year in Korea. January 1, *Seolial*, is a national holiday based on the Western calendar, when Koreans celebrate with the rest of the world. Koreans also observe the Lunar New Year,

On New Year's Eve, 2010, a South Korean diver dressed as a rabbit holds a sign reading "Happy New Year" in a fish tank to welcome the upcoming year at the COEX Aquarium in Seoul. The year 2011 was the Year of the Rabbit.

or *Daeboreum*, a time when they can enjoy three days off work or school. This occurs on the first full moon of the first month in the new year.

Younger Koreans generally consider January 1 the start of the new year. Their elders, however, put greater emphasis on lunar dates and mark the start of the new year on the lunar calendar. In the West, Passover and Easter are examples of holidays that occur on or after the full moon after the spring equinox.

A lot of preparation precedes the Lunar New Year. Homes are cleaned and debts repaid. The focus of the festival is the honoring of one's elders and ancestors. Children wear new hanbok and socks and shoes to bow and offer their respects to their parents and grandparents, who in turn give them their blessings and money or other small gifts. People send one another greeting cards and exchange simple handmade gifts during the Lunar New Year.

Family gatherings and visiting friends are also important activities during the Lunar New Year. Cousins, aunts, uncles, and other relatives come together at the home of the eldest member of the extended family for a memorial service to their dead ancestors, a tradition originating in Buddhism. Food is prepared and set in front of photographs of the deceased. Everyone bows to the photographs, and then the younger people bow to their eldest living relatives.

Over the next few days, Koreans visit other people to whom respect is due. For example, employees visit their bosses, students visit their teachers, and so on.

THE FIRST FULL MOON

Dae-bo-rum, or "the first full moon," is celebrated on full moon in the first month of the year. In the past, the Korean New Year festivities ended on Dae-bo-rum.

Koreans have always been fascinated by the moon. Farmers believed they could predict the weather for the coming months by the color of the first full moon. A golden moon foretold perfect weather, and a reddish moon meant little rain.

Koreans traditionally believe that catching a glimpse of the first full moon rising brings good luck for the coming year. People gather in the afternoon, often on a hilltop, to wait to see the rim of the rising moon. Those in the countryside light little mounds of twigs to signal the momentous event.

The first full moon is a very cheerful and rousing time in Korea. Neighboring villages engage in tug-of-war competitions and mock torch fights and stone fights. Youths spend the day searching for good-luck charms and doing things nine times for good luck.

Special Dae-bo-rum foods include peanuts, chestnuts, and walnuts (*Bureom*). It is thought that such foods will keep one's skin clear the whole year. A dish called *ogokpap* (OH-gohk-pahp), made of five different rice grains, is a traditional offering during this festival.

Visitors enjoy the cherry blossoms at the Yeouido Spring Flower Festival.

CHERRY BLOSSOM FESTIVAL

When spring begins in Korea in early April, the cherry trees bloom, and their pretty pink flowers fill the air with a sweet scent. So lovely are the cherry trees in spring that people go out for the whole day just to enjoy the beauty of the cherry blossom festival. The city of Jinhae hosts a ten day celebration of the blossoms. Over one million visitors crowd into town to see the cherry

Buddhists march on the street as they prepare for the Buddha's birthday in Seoul.

blossoms, as well as street performers, carnival stalls, military parades and night time light shows.

The Japanese planted Korea's first cherry trees in Jinhae, during the colonial occupation (1910—1945), where they had their naval headquarters. At the end of World War II, when the Japanese surrendered and the South Koreans gained independence, most of the cherry trees in Korea were uprooted, because they reminded the Koreans of the Japanese.

New cherry trees have since been planted in Jinhae, and the cherry blossom festival continues to be enjoyed but with a different focus. Koreans now celebrate the festival in honor of the famed Admiral Yi Sunsin, who in the sixteenth century defeated Japanese soldiers in the Imjin War.

THE BUDDHA'S BIRTHDAY

The Buddha's birthday is celebrated on the eighth day of the fourth lunar month, which is sometime between late April and late May. On that day, Buddhists attend some of the numerous religious ceremonies and events held at temples throughout the country.

Once the state religion of the Korean peninsula, Buddhism fell from favor during the Joseon dynasty. It was then that Confucianism replaced it as a social force. In spite of that, Buddhism still ranks as one of the main religions of Korea.

On the Buddha's birthday, colorful paper lanterns and flowers adorn the courtyards of temples, and tags printed with the names of people's ancestors hang from the lanterns. Koreans congregate at the temples to offer their prayers and ask for the Buddha's blessing. Many bring homemade lanterns. Others bring flowers to the altar of the Buddha or burn incense before the altar. The day culminates with an evening parade of candlelit lanterns. The light symbolizes hope.

CHILDREN'S DAY

South Koreans celebrate Children's Day on May 5. The holiday originated during the Japanese occupation of Korea. It replaced what was previously Boys' Day, reflecting a social consciousness that all children, not just boys, should be treasured.

On Children's Day, Korean children receive gifts from their parents. They often wear their traditional dress when visiting the many public pageants and martial-arts demonstrations held in their honor.

DANO DAY

Koreans have celebrated Dano Day, also known as Swing Day, for centuries. This celebration of spring and farming falls on the fifth day of the fifth lunar month—generally sometime between late May and late June.

This festival originated as a day to pray for good harvests and is especially important among people living in rural areas. According to ancient records, farming activity stopped on Dano Day, and there were festivities similar to those of the Lunar New Year.

Dano Day is usually celebrated outdoors. People in villages assemble in the village square, marketplace, or other common space, while people in cities gather in parks and other open-air event venues to watch and take part in the day's festivities. There are puppet shows, wrestling matches, swinging contests, and a whole lot of dancing. Many of the events have their origin in the ancient celebration of the Dano festival when it was not often that women were allowed to leave the confines of their homes and celebrate in the presence of men.

Men display their strength in wrestling, or *ssireum*, matches, and the winner gets a bull as a prize. Women take part in swinging contests. The villages usually set up a long swing on the branch of an old tree, and the women of the town compete to see who can swing the highest standing up. The winner sometimes gets a gold ring. Mask dances are performed in some regions to drive away evil spirits. On Dano, People eat traditional foods including a variety of *tteok*, a type of rice cake that can be either sweet or savory. UNESCO has designated the "Gangneung Dano-je Festival as a "Masterpiece of the Oral and Intangible Heritage of Humanity."

THE HARVEST MOON

Chuseok, the harvest moon, is celebrated on the fifteenth day of the eighth lunar month, when the moon is brightest, sometime between early September and early October. Also known as *Hangawi*, the Korean thanksgiving, families return to their ancestral homes to attend memorial ceremonies in honor of their ancestors. Like many other harvest festivals, it is held around the Autumn Equinox and is celebrated for three consecutive days.

One of the major foods prepared and eaten during the Chuseok holiday is *songpyeon*, a Korean traditional rice cake which contains stuffing made with healthy ingredients such as sesame seeds, black beans, mung beans, cinnamon, pine nut, walnut, chestnut, jujube, and honey. The word "*song*" in *songpyeon* means a pine tree in Korean. After the feast, some Koreans dress in traditional clothing and visit graves to make food offerings and bow to their ancestors.

Koreans have long believed that the moon inspires creativity. In the early days, the harvest moon festivities usually ended with the viewing of the full moon and poetry reading and writing.

CHRISTMAS

Christmas is an official holiday in Korea, with almost one-third of South Koreans being Christians. People attend Christmas church services during the season and reflect on the significance of the birth of Jesus Christ and thank God for the gift of His son. Commercially, Christmas in Korea is similar to Christmas in the West. People decorate their homes, sing carols, shop for gifts in stores with elaborate displays, and enjoy festive feasts. Santa Claus can also be seen around Korea but instead of wearing red, he might be in blue! He's also known as *Santa Kullosu* or Santa Grandfather. Finding a Christmas tree in Seoul to bring home and decorate is not possible though.

KOREA'S CALENDAR OF OFFICIAL HOLIDAYS

Many of South Korea's festivals are derived from the agricultural cycle. For centuries, farmers planted and harvested on special days, which were marked on the lunar calendar based on the phases and positions of the moon. These festivals continue to be celebrated today, but not all of them can be declared public holidays. A list of South Korea's official holidays follows.

January 1	New Year's Day
January	Lunar New Year (Seollal)
March 1	Independence Movement Day
April/May	(8th day of the 4th lunar month) Buddha's birthday
April 5	Arbor Day
May 5	Children's Day
June 6	Memorial Day, a day of tribute to the war dead
July 17	Constitution Day
August 15	Liberation Day, the anniversary of liberation from Japan in 1945
September/October	Chuseok (Thanksgiving)
October 3	National Foundation Day, or Dangun Day, the traditional founding of Korea by Dangun in 2333 BCE
December 25	Christmas Day

INTERNET LINKS

www.timeanddate.com/holidays/south-korea/
Holidays in Korea by date each year.

english.visitkorea.or.kr/enu/AK/AK_EN_1_5_2.jsp
The official site of Korean Tourism has a page devoted to holidays and the calendar.

Shoppers visit the Foot-Long Ice Cream Cone Shop in Seoul.

13

KOREA'S LONG TRADITION OF FOOD preparation and eating, which dates back thousands of years, is closely tied to good health and spiritual well being.

Koreans eat three meals a day, but breakfast, lunch, and dinner foods are similar. The difference is the number of side dishes, or *banchan* (bun-CHAHN). As many as six side dishes are served for breakfast, a dozen for lunch, and nearly twenty for dinner.

Each meal generally includes rice, a traditional Korean pickle called *kimchi* (KIM-chee), and soup, which doubles as a drink, and a seasonal fruit closes the meal. Traditionally, Korean food is served in small bowls

A tempting display of small dishes, or banchan, are arranged on a low dining table.

Bosintang is a traditional Korean soup made with dog meat. The name means "invigorating soup," as dog meat is thought to have cooling qualities in the summer heat. A special breed, the *nureongi*, is bred for its meat; pet dogs are generally not used. Today the custom is controversial and many South Koreans—particularly young people—disapprove.

Soup, such as this one with rice dumplings, is an important part of a Korean meal.

that are neatly arranged on a low table. All dishes are served at the same time; there is no tradition of different courses, as in Western dining.

Korean soups contain several ingredients such as beef, tofu, mung beans, and vegetables. There are special soups for special occasions, such as weddings, births, and New Year celebrations. Red pepper, green onion, garlic, sesame oil, and soy sauce give Korean food a strong aroma and make it easily identifiable among other Asian cuisines.

BANCHAN

Side dishes, or *banchan*, add an interesting dimension to Korean meals. Usually prepared with a combination of spices and sauces, such as soy sauce, sesame oil, chilies, garlic, and ginger, side dishes complement the main course of rice or noodles by giving it flavor. Almost any food can be eaten as a side dish, but some side dishes are more popular than others and are also served in bars as cocktail hors d'oeuvres called *anju* (AHN-joo).

The most famous Korean side dish is the indispensable kimchi. Other favorites include different meats as well as a variety of vegetables. One of the best-known meat-based banchan consists of beef strips seasoned in soy sauce, sesame oil, garlic, and chili pepper, and grilled. Broiled seasoned pork ribs are also popular. The grilled beef, called *bulgogi*, has become popular in the United States and other Western countries as more and more people discover Korean food in local restaurants.

Vegetable- and seafood-based alternatives include: blanched spinach with sesame oil and sesame seeds; fish cakes, sliced raw fish, sautéed oysters; sautéed dried anchovies; raw crab legs soaked in red-pepper sauce; and tofu seasoned and cooked in an endless number of ways.

KIMCHI

Kimchi is Korea's signature dish of spicy, pickled vegetables. Said to be high in vitamins and nutrients, the fermented delicacy is eaten at every meal with rice. Kimchi is closely associated with the national identity.

Kimchi ferments without vinegar, and the predominant flavor is red pepper. There are probably more than two hundred varieties of kimchi, but mainly two varieties are eaten in all Korean homes: whole cabbage and hard radish. The whole cabbage variety consists of salted cabbage, sliced vegetables, herbs and spices, fermented fish sauce, fresh oysters, garlic, and chilies. The hard radish variety consists of cubed radish, sliced cabbage, and a few other kinds of vegetables.

Volunteers make tons of kimchi for the needy in a park in Seoul in November 2012.

In summer, kimchi is prepared weekly, since the vegetables are in season. But when winter sets in, no crops can be produced until late spring. The approach of winter marks the start of a long kimchi-making time called *gimjang* (KIM-jahng). Before November ends, when the weather has cooled and the crops are in from the fields, the outdoor markets are burgeoning. Koreans start slicing and spicing, preparing enough kimchi to last through winter.

During gimjang, Koreans gather in groups to cut, wash, and salt hundreds of pounds of cabbage and white radish. After it is prepared, kimchi is stored in the yard in large earthen-ware crocks. In the countryside, the crocks are buried up to their necks to keep the pickled vegetables from freezing.

While refrigerators are now widely available in Korea, many people still follow the gimjang tradition that has been passed down to them from older generations. Even Koreans living in the big cities store crocks of kimchi on the balcony of their apartment.

HEALTH AND FOOD

The popularity of bulgogi, bibimbap, kimchi, and other Korean food is on the rise. Drawing on millennia of culinary wisdom, Koreans enjoy good health and very low rates of obesity due to the central place vegetables have in the Korean diet. Whereas 30.6 percent of Americans are considered obese, the highest percentage in the world; only 3.2 percent of Koreans are overweight, the lowest percentage in the world, along with Japan, also 3.2 percent.

A man sells traditional street food, such as fish ball sticks, at the Insadong Market in Seoul.

FOOD AS MEDICINE Koreans know that good food is important to having a sound body and mind. Most Korean meals have less than six hundred calories. Soup is always part of a meal and helps fill the stomach. Meat is eaten in more moderation and isn't the main ingredient in a meal. Kimchi is loaded with minerals, vitamins, and fiber. Hot chili often accompanies a meal and is known to increase the metabolism, helping to burn off calories.

Vegetables play a central role in the meal. Cabbage and other leafy vegetables, mushrooms, and potatoes are popular. Sweet, calorie-laden desserts are not found much in Korea. Instead, most people find a bit of fresh orange or watermelon to be the perfect way to end a meal. A teen's perfect snack may not be a bag of salty, fried chips but instead a cooked squid. However, as Western fast food chains are making inroads in Korean cities, the rate of obesity is beginning to rise with burgers and chips making their way into daily diets.

YIN/YANG AND THE FIVE ELEMENTS Korean cuisine embraces a philosophy of *Eumyangohaeng*. Food must balance in color and relate to the five elements. First, *Yin-qi* and *Yang-qi* are created to represent sky and earth. From these come wood, fire, earth, metal, and water. White and yellow foods have Yin-qi and blue (green) and black have Yang-qi. The five elements are represented by five colors and directions, including center. White rice is topped by foods having a balance of colors.

Eumyangohaeng encompasses more than good eating; it is a whole philosophy of life. The five elements also relate to the seasons, body parts, intelligence, and emotions.

TABLE MANNERS

Each diner is equipped with a pair of chopsticks and a soup spoon. Once the meal begins, the chopsticks never touch the table. Neither are they ever stuck straight up in the rice. Instead, the diner rests his or her chopsticks across the rice bowl. First, one tastes the soup or kimchi juice, then tries the rice or other dishes. It is rude to make noise with the spoon or chopsticks hitting the bowl.

Eating with the elderly has special rules. The eldest person gets the place at the table farthest from the door, as it is considered the best spot. No one starts eating until the eldest person picks up the spoon. In the company of the elderly, one must sit upright, not slouch, and rise when the older person gets up after a meal is finished.

Rice is served in individual bowls, and each person is expected to finish his or her serving. The side dishes are shared by everyone. Koreans never use their fingers to pick up food, and it is the height of bad manners to read a book or magazine or watch TV while eating.

ENTERTAINING GUESTS

Koreans spare no expense in entertaining guests in their homes. They consider it a matter of great pride to make the home comfortable and to prepare a special meal that is pleasing to their guests.

Korean beef noodle soup with prawn tempura

FAST FOOD DELIVERY

Many fast food restaurants in Korea will deliver straight to one's home using motorcycle drivers who are known for speeding through city traffic to get the food delivered quickly. McDonald's, for instance, delivers twenty-four hours a day ... even at 5:00 in the morning. Some of the Korean McDonald's specialties include the Bulgogi Burger and the Shanghai Spicy Chicken Burger.

The meal is usually preceded by drinks served in the living room. The guests are then invited to eat in the dining area. In traditional homes, low tables are placed end to end and laid out with all the dishes that have been prepared for the meal.

Before the meal begins, the host will usually tell the guests to eat as much as they want even though the meal is humble. This reflects the Korean belief that even the most sumptuous food is never good enough for honored guests. The host greatly appreciates it if the guests ask for more food, since it is a sign that they are enjoying the food.

However, despite the host's urging to eat a lot, the guests will always leave a little food in their rice bowls at the end of the meal. This serves to assure the host that enough food has been served and the guests have had their fill.

Koreans traditionally do not talk much during meals. Instead, they concentrate on relishing the taste of the food. When the guests have finished, the host will clear the table and serve coffee and seasonal fruit. The host is prepared to entertain the guests for hours, especially when alcohol is served.

ALCOHOLIC DRINKS

South Korea's drinking culture reveals much about its social structure, culture, and traditions. Manners are very important to Koreans and most were established by the 1300s. During the Confucian Joseon period, scholars would get together for educational sessions called *Hyanguemjurye* where the drinking of alcohol was an important part of the occasion. Drinking with elders is a sign of respect and one of the biggest compliments a Korean worker can receive is to be invited out for a drink by the boss.

Koreans follow strict rules when drinking. They never pour alcoholic drinks for themselves but for others. Someone of lower status will offer a glass to someone of higher status, and if the status or age difference is significant, the person receiving the glass as well as the person offering it will either use both hands or hold the glass in the right hand supported by the left. When the glass reaches the receiver's hand, the giver pours the alcohol into it.

It is the custom to pass one's glass on until everyone has exchanged glasses with everyone else. Drinkers do not pour alcohol into a partially filled glass. There is no problem if someone chooses not to drink, but that person will take the offered drink and just let it sit at their side rather than refuse it. In Korea, alcohol is everywhere and it is inexpensive.

INTERNET LINKS

www.lifeinkorea.com/food/f-manners.cfm
Information about table manners from the Life in Korea cultural site.

seoulistic.com/korean-culture/drinking-culture-in-south-korea-and-why-its-important/
All about the drinking culture in Korea.

www.koreaherald.com/view.php?ud=20100603000599
Colors, meanings, charms, and flavors in Korean dishes from *The Korean Herald*.

KOREAN RICE BOWL

This is a simplified, somewhat Westernized version of bibimbap, a Korean dish made of rice topped with vegetables, sliced meat, a fried egg, and hot sauce.

1 ½ pounds trimmed flank or strip steak, very thinly sliced

¼ cup soy sauce

3 tablespoons (Tbsp) Asian sesame oil, divided

2 green onions, finely chopped

2 Tbsp sugar

1 Tbsp sake or dry Sherry

1 garlic clove, minced

1 ½ pounds fresh vegetables; choose three of different colors: slender asparagus spears, shredded cabbage, thin carrot matchsticks, bell pepper strips, zucchini sticks, spinach, mung bean sprouts (keep vegetables separate)

2 teaspoons (tsp) vegetable oil plus additional for pan

6 large eggs

6 cups freshly cooked short-grain white rice

Toasted sesame seeds, Korean hot pepper paste (*kochujang*), kimchi

Whisk soy sauce, 2 tablespoons sesame oil, green onions, sugar, sake, and garlic in medium bowl. Marinate steak in soy mixture at room temperature 30 minutes.

On baking sheet, toss veggies lightly with vegetable oil, keeping each type separate. In skillet, sauté veggies in separate batches until crisp-tender, about 2—4 minutes each. Sprouts will take a few seconds. Return to baking sheet and sprinkle with sesame oil. Keep warm.

Brush skillet with vegetable oil. Working in batches, grill steak until just browned, about 1 minute per side. Transfer to bowl; keep warm. Add another tablespoon of vegetable oil to pan. Crack eggs into pan and cook until whites are set but yolks are still runny, 2 to 3 minutes.

Divide warm rice among bowls. Place beef on top of rice; arrange veggies next to steak. Top with fried egg. Sprinkle with sesame seeds; serve with Korean hot pepper paste or hot sauce and kimchi.

DAK GOMTANG (KOREAN CHICKEN SOUP)

1 whole chicken (3—4 pounds)
10—12 garlic cloves
1 oz piece ginger
½ medium onion
2—3 scallion white parts
½ tsp whole black peppers
¼ tsp white pepper
3 quarts water
1 Tbsp soy sauce
cooked white rice, about ½ cup
    per person
3 scallions, finely chopped to garnish
salt and pepper to taste

Place the cleaned chicken in a stock pot. Add the garlic, ginger, onion, scallions, peppers and 10 cups of water (or enough to cover the chicken).

Bring to a boil over high heat. Skim off any foam on top. Reduce the heat to medium low and simmer, covered, for about one hour.

Turn the heat off and carefully remove the chicken, and break apart to speed cooling. When the chicken is cool enough to handle, remove the meat from the bones. Shred the meat into small bite size pieces. Return the bones back to the broth and simmer again for another hour.

Strain the broth and remove the excess fat. To serve, place some rice in a serving bowl, add chicken pieces, and then ladle the hot broth on top. Pass chopped scallions, salt and pepper separately so each person can season to taste. Serve hot with kimchi.

A   **B**   **C**   **D**

RUSSIA

- ● Capital city
- • Major town
- ▲ Mountain peak

Feet	Meters
16,500	5,000
9,900	3,000
6,600	2,000
3,300	1,000
1,650	500
660	200
0	0

1

C H I N A

Tumen

Mount Paektu
(9,003 ft/2,743 m)

NORTH
HAMGYONG

• Chongjin

Yalu

Changjin

YANGGANG

Hamgyong Mountains

CHAGANG

Kangnam Mountains

Kaema Plateau

2

Nangnim Mountains

SOUTH
HAMGYONG

• Kimchaek

NORTH
PYONGAN

NORTH

KOREA

• Sinpo

• Hamhung

E a s t

S e a

SOUTH
PYONGAN

Pyongyang ●
PYONGYANG

• Wonsan

K o r e a

B a y

NAMPO

NORTH
HWANGHAE

KANGWON

Mount
Geumgang ▲

Taebaek

SOUTH
HWANGHAE

KAESONG

Mount Seorak ▲

3

Kaesong • ● Panmunjeom

• Pocheon

▲ Mount Odae

Incheon ●
INCHEON

Seoul ●
SEOUL

KANGWON

Mountains

Han

KYONGGI

NORTH
CHUNGCHONG

N

SOUTH
CHUNGCHONG

Y e l l o w

S e a

Taejon •

NORTH
KYONGSANG

SOUTH

KOREA

Sobaek Mountains

Naktong

4

Geumsan •

Daegu •

• Pohang

NORTH
CHOLLA

• Gyeongju

• Ulsan

Kwangju •

Hadong •

SOUTH KYONGSANG

Masan •

Jinhae • ● Busan
BUSAN

SOUTH
CHOLLA

Korea Strait

J A P A N

5

Jin

Jeju • JEJU
Mount Halla ▲
(6,398 ft / 1,949 m) *Jeju Island*

MAP OF KOREA

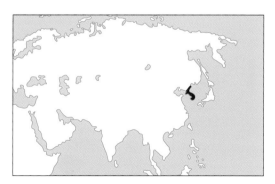

ECONOMIC KOREA

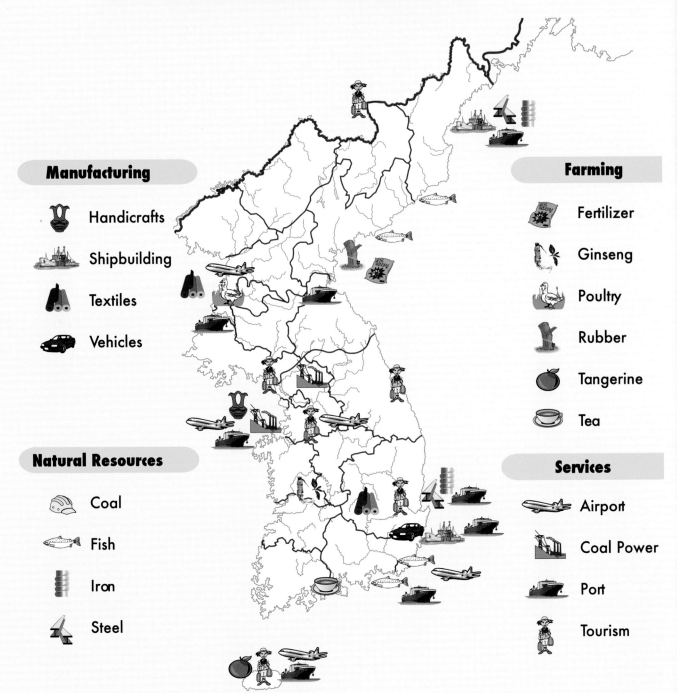

Manufacturing

- Handicrafts
- Shipbuilding
- Textiles
- Vehicles

Natural Resources

- Coal
- Fish
- Iron
- Steel

Farming

- Fertilizer
- Ginseng
- Poultry
- Rubber
- Tangerine
- Tea

Services

- Airport
- Coal Power
- Port
- Tourism

ABOUT THE ECONOMY

OVERVIEW

South Korea's economy grew at a remarkable rate over the past forty years, becoming a global high tech industrialized economy. South Korea is currently the 12th largest economy in the world. Challenges to the economy in the future include an aging population, a heavy dependence on exports, and an inflexible labor market.

GROSS DOMESTIC PRODUCT (GDP)

US $1.666 trillion, 2013 estimate

GDP SECTORS

agriculture 2.6 percent, industry 39.2 percent, services 58.2 percent (2013)

AGRICULTURAL PRODUCTS

barley, cattle, eggs, fish, fruit, milk, pork, poultry, rice, root crops, vegetables

INDUSTRIAL PRODUCTS

clothing, footwear, electronic products, ships, steel, textiles, vehicles

CURRENCY

South Korean won (KRW)
USD 1 = KRW 1,107.3 (2013)

WORKFORCE

22 million (agriculture 9.5 percent, industry 21.5 percent, services 69 percent)

MAJOR TRADE PARTNERS

United States, Japan, China, Hong Kong, Singapore

MAJOR EXPORTS

semiconductors, wireless telecommunications equipment, motor vehicles, auto parts, computers, display, home appliances, wire telecommunication equipment, steel, ships, petrochemicals.

MAJOR PORTS

Incheon, Pohang, Busan, Ulsan, Yeosu, Kwangyang

INTERNATIONAL AIRPORTS

South: Incheon, Yangyang, Busan, Jeju

South Korea

North Korea

CULTURAL KOREA

Kim Il Sung Square
Pyongyang's center boasts a square similar to China's Tiananmen. Surrounded by important government buildings, Kim Il Sung Square has beautiful views of the Taedong River.

Kaesong
The old capital of the Goryeo dynasty is home to a museum of celadon pottery and other Confucian relics. The city also preserves a traditional Korean atmosphere and natural landscapes such as the Pakyon Falls.

Demilitarized Zone
Panmunjeom is located in the demilitarized zone and is an important venue for peace talks between North and South Korea. Soldiers guard both sides of the border, and civilians need a permit to visit the area.

Ceramics Village
In Incheon, at one of Korea's largest ceramics villages, visitors can buy beautiful quality ceramics as well as learn the art of traditional pottery.

Lake of Heaven
The tallest mountain in the Korean peninsula has a snow-covered peak, or "white head," throughout the year. Mount Paektu's crater contains one of the world's deepest alpine lakes: Cheonji, or Lake of Heaven, up to 1,260 feet (394 m) deep.

Mountain Gateway
The Geumgang mountains are home to waterfalls, mineral springs, temples, and a museum. The mountains are the only place where South Koreans can enter North Korea.

Ski Resorts
Both professional and amateur skiers patronize the resorts in Gangwon province from December to March to enjoy South Korea's snowy slopes in winter.

Ancient Palaces
Seoul's five main palaces were built as early as the 15th century. The preserved ruins continue to draw visitors to admire its architecture, gardens, and relics.

Grandfathers of Jeju
Formed from lava deposits, Jeju Island has breathtaking natural volcanic rock structures and more than 40 statues called grandfathers, which are believed to be more than 200 years old.

Gyeongju
The old capital of the Silla dynasty is known as a museum without walls. Its many well-preserved sites include the ancient tombs of Cheonmachong (Flying Horse Tomb).

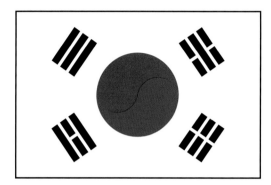

COUNTRY NAME
conventional long form: Republic of Korea
conventional short form: South Korea
local long form: Taehan-min'guk
local short form: Han'guk
abbreviation: ROK

GOVERNMENT TYPE
Republic

CAPITAL
Seoul, 9.736 Million

OTHER MAJOR CITIES
Busan, Daegu, Incheon, Ulsan

NATIONAL FLAG
white, with black trigrams from the I Ching (Book of Changes) and a red and blue yin-yang symbol

NATIONAL ANTHEM
"Aegukga" (Patriotic Song), adopted in 1948

POPULATION
49,039,986 (July 2014 est.)

OFFICIAL LANGUAGE
Korean

NATIONAL SYMBOL
taegeuk (yin yang symbol)

ETHNIC GROUPS
most are ethnic Koreans; small percentage are ethnic Chinese

RELIGIOUS GROUPS
Christian 31.6 percent (Protestant 24 percent, Roman Catholic 7.6 percent), Buddhist 24.2 percent, other or unknown 0.9 percent, none 43.3 percent (2010)

LEADERS IN POLITICS
chief of state: President PARK Geun-hye (February 2013)
head of government: (vacant); note -Prime Minister CHUNG Hong-won resigned April 27, 2014; MOON Chang-keuk was nominated Prime Minister June 10, 2014 and awaits parliamentary confirmation; Deputy Prime Minister HYUN Oh-seok (June 2013)

OTHER FAMOUS KOREANS
Ban Ki-moon, eighth Secretary-General of the United Nations, Lee Kang-baek, Korean playwright, Nam June Paik (video artist), Sun Myung Moon — Founder of the Unification Church, Kim Yong-ok, philosopher, Ryu, Hyun-Jin Professional baseball player, currently playing in Los Angeles Dodgers, MLB, Andrew Kim Taegon, was the first Korean-born Catholic priest and Canonized Saint

TIMELINE

IN KOREA	IN THE WORLD

6,000 BCE
Neolithic peoples arrive.

753 BCE
Rome is founded.

108 BCE
China's Han dynasty establishes four territories on the peninsula.

116–117 BCE
The Roman Empire reaches its greatest extent.

57–18 BCE
The Silla, Goguryeo, and Baekje kingdoms are founded.

668 CE
Goguryeo and Baekje are unified under Silla.

600 CE
Height of Mayan civilization

918
Wang Kon founds Goryeo.

1000
The Chinese perfect gunpowder and begin to use it in warfare.

1231
Mongols invade Goryeo.

1392
Yi Seong-gye founds the Joseon dynasty.

1558–1603
Reign of Elizabeth I of England

1592
Japan invades Korea.

1598
Korea drives out Japan with China's help.

1620
Pilgrims sail the *Mayflower* to America.

1776
U.S. Declaration of Independence signed.

1861
The U.S. Civil War begins.

1910
Japan annexes Korea.

1914
World War I begins.

1939
World War II begins.

1945
The peninsula is divided. Soviet troops occupy the north, U.S. troops the south.

1945
World War II ends.

IN KOREA	IN THE WORLD
1948 Syngman Rhee is elected president of South Korea; Kim Il-Sung leads North Korea.	**1949** The North Atlantic Treaty Organization (NATO) is formed.
1950–53 The Korean War	**1957** The Russians launch *Sputnik*.
1960–61 Riots force Rhee to resign. Park Chung Hee stages a coup and imposes martial law.	**1966–1969** The Chinese Cultural Revolution
1979 Park is assassinated.	
1988 Seoul hosts the Olympic Games.	**1986** Nuclear power disaster at Chernobyl in Ukraine
1991 Both Koreas join the United Nations.	**1991** Breakup of the Soviet Union
1994 Kim Jong-Il succeeds the late Kim Il-Sung.	
1998 Kim Dae Jung engages North Korea with the Sunshine Policy.	**1997** Britain returns Hong Kong to China
2000 Kim Dae Jung and Kim Jong-Il meet. Families separated by the border reunite. Kim Dae Jung wins the Nobel Peace Prize.	**2001** Terrorists crash planes in New York, Washington, D.C., and Pennsylvania.
2002 South Korea hosts the World Cup.	
2003 North Korea continues its nuclear program in violation of international agreements.	**2003** War in Iraq
2010 Japan apologizes to South Korea for colonization on the 100th anniversary of Japan's annexation of the Korean Peninsula in 1910.	**2008** United States elects first black president, Barack Obama. **2013** Francis I becomes pope, the first pope from the Americas.
2014 *MW Sewol*, a South Korean ferry carrying 476 people, mostly high school students, sinks en route to the island of Jeju, killing some 300 people.	**2014** Hostilities erupt between Israel and Hamas-led Gaza Strip

GLOSSARY

banchan (bun-CHAHN)
The side dishes that accompany a Korean meal.

beomjong
A Buddhist bell.

chaebol (JAE-bull)
A business conglomerate.

chungmae (choong-MAY)
An arranged marriage.

dol (DOUL)
A child's first birthday.

haenyeo (hay-NIO)
A dwindling group of women divers preserving a more than 1,500-year-old tradition in Jeju.

ham (HAHM)
A box of gifts for the bride, sent by the groom as part of the Korean wedding ritual.

hanbok (HUN-bok)
The traditional Korean dress.

hangeul (HAHN-gool)
The Korean phonetic writing system.

hwangap (HWUN-gup)
A person's sixtieth birthday.

insam (in-SUM)
Ginseng, a herb believed to be a cure-all and consumed as a health tonic.

juche (CHOO-cheh)
Self-reliance.

kibun (KEY-boon)
Social harmony.

kimchi (KIM-chee)
A traditional Korean pickle.

kisaeng (KEY-sang)
A female entertainer, usually a talented poet, singer, or musician.

kumjul (KEHM-jool)
A straw rope of chili peppers hung across the doorway of a house to frighten off evil spirits and warn people not to enter because a baby has just been born.

mudang (MOO-dung)
A shaman, or spirit medium.

nunchi (NOON-chi)
An intuition or hunch that enables a person to read another person's state of mind.

ondol (ON-doll)
A system of pipes beneath the floor of a house that carry warm air from the kitchen stove.

Samsin Halmeoni (SUM-sin Hul-MO-neh)
The grandmother spirit associated with childbirth.

Seollal (SUHL-lahl)
The Lunar New Year.

sijo (SAE-jo)
A form of traditional Korean poetry.

FOR FURTHER INFORMATION

Books

DK Publishing, *Top 10 Seoul* (Eyewitness Top 10 Travel Guide), New York, NY: DK Travel/Penguin Random House, 2013.

Hong, Euny. *The Birth of Korean Cool: How One Nation Is Conquering the World Through Pop Culture.* London, England: Picador, 2014.

Kim, Richard E. *Lost Names: Scenes from a Korean Boyhood.* Oakland, CA: University of California Press, 1970; reissued in 2011 with new preface.

Lee, Cecilia Hae-Jin. *Quick and Easy Korean Cooking.* San Francisco, CA: Chronicle Books, 2009.

Lonely Planet, and Simon Richmond. *Lonely Planet Korea*, Travel Guide 9th edition. Oakland, CA: Lonely Planet, 2013

Myers, B. R. *The Cleanest Race: How North Koreans See Themselves and Why It Matters.* New York, NY: Melville House, reprint edition, 2011.

Videos

Families of Korea. Families of the World VHS Series. Master Communications, 2001.

Hidden Korea. PBS Home Video, 2001.

Websites

BBC News Asia. South Korea profile/Timeline. www.bbc.com/news/world-asia-pacific-15292674

The Chosun Ilbo, english.chosun.com

Korea.net: The official website of the Republic of Korea. www.korea.net

Korea.net: The official website of the Republic of Korea. www.korea.net

The Korea Times. www.koreatimes.co.kr

Korea Tourism Organization, "Imagine Your Korea." english.visitkorea.or.kr

BIBLIOGRAPHY

Central Intelligence Agency, "The World Factbook." www.cia.gov/library/publications/the-world-factbook/geos/ks.html

Heritage Foundation, the, "2014 Index of Economic Freedom." www.heritage.org/index/country/northkorea

Hudson, Gavin. "Korean Tigers Back From Extinction but Not in South Korea." Ecolocalizer.com. Nov. 24, 2008. ecolocalizer.com/2008/11/24/korean-tigers-back-from-the-brink-of-extinction-but-not-in-south-korea

Kantor, Jodi. "A Look at Korea's Culture From the Bathhouse." *New York Times*, Feb. 7, 2014 www.nytimes.com/2014/02/09/travel/a-look-at-koreas-culture-from-the-bathhouse.html

Koo, Se-Woong. "An Assault Upon Our Children." *New York Times*, Aug. 1, 2014 www.nytimes.com/2014/08/02/opinion/sunday/south-koreas-education-system-hurts-students.html?hp&action=click&pgtype=Homepage&module=c-column-top-span-region&region=c-column-top-span-region&WT.nav=c-column-top-span-region&_r=2

Kwon, Michelle. "South Korea's Woeful Workplace Inequality." *The Diplomat*, May 3, 2014 thediplomat.com/2014/05/south-koreas-woeful-workplace-inequality

Lee, Chung Min. "The Legacies of Kim Dae-jung." *Wall Street Journal*, Aug. 19, 2009 online.wsj.com/news/articles/SB10001424052970203550604574359963735575736

Lee, Ji-nu, and Kim Yi-Jeong. "Korean Buddhist Bells," *Templestay*, Winter 2013 eng.templestay.com/upload/board/2013121810273680997.pdf

Macintyre, Donald. "For One Old Soldier, The Battle Is Over." *Time*, Dec. 12, 2002 content.time.com/time/magazine/article/0,9171,395415,00.html

Manyin, Mark E., and Mary Beth D. Nikitin. "Foreign Assistance to North Korea." Congressional Research Service, April 2, 2014 fas.org/sgp/crs/row/R40095.pdf

O'Neill, Tom. "Korea's DMZ: Dangerous Divide." *National Geographic*, July 2003. ngm.nationalgeographic.com/features/world/asia/north-korea/dmz-text/1

Rauhala, Emily. "20 Years After His Death, Kim Il Sung Still Casts a Powerful Spell Over North Korea." *Time*, July 8, 2014. time.com/2964757/north-korea-kim-il-sung-20-years-anniversary

Religion Facts. "Confucianism." www.religionfacts.com/a-z-religion-index/confucianism.htm

Shin, Gi-Wook. "Ethnic pride source of prejudice, discrimination." *The Korea Herald,* August 2, 2006, accessed through Stanford University Asia-Pacific Research Center. aparc.stanford.edu/news/koreas_ethnic_nationalism_is_a_source_of_both_pride_and_prejudice_according_to_giwook_shin_20060802

UNESCO World Heritage. Republic of Korea. whc.unesco.org/en/statesparties/kr

INDEX

INDEX